M000200543

When LIFE
Doesn't Make
SENSE

Books by Leslie Haskin

FROM BETHANY HOUSE PUBLISHERS

Between Heaven and Ground Zero
God Has Not Forgotten About You
When Life Doesn't Make Sense

When LIFE Doesn't Make SENSE

Real Answers for Tough Times and Tough Questions

LESLIE HASKIN

BETHANY HOUSE PUBLISHERS
a division of Baker Publishing Group
Minneapolis, Minnesota

© 2012 by Leslie Haskin

Published by Bethany House Publishers
11400 Hampshire Avenue South
Bloomington, Minnesota 55438
www.bethanyhouse.com

Bethany House Publishers is a division of
Baker Publishing Group, Grand Rapids, Michigan

Printed in the United States of America

All rights reserved. No part of this publication may be reproduced, stored in a retrieval system, or transmitted in any form or by any means—for example, electronic, photocopy, recording—without the prior written permission of the publisher. The only exception is brief quotations in printed reviews.

Library of Congress Cataloging-in-Publication Data
Haskin, Leslie D.
    When life doesn't make sense : real answers for tough times and tough questions / Leslie Haskin.
        p. cm.
    ISBN 978-0-7642-0995-6 (pbk. : alk. paper)
    1. Christian life. 2. Spiritual life—Christianity. I. Title.
    BV4501.3.H377 2012
    248.8'6—dc23   2012006415

Unless otherwise indicated, Scripture quotations are from the Holy Bible, New International Version®. NIV®. Copyright © 1973, 1978, 1984, 2011 by Biblica, Inc.™ Used by permission of Zondervan. All rights reserved worldwide. www.zondervan.com

Scripture quotations identified KJV are from the King James Version of the Bible.

Scripture quotations marked NKJV are from the New King James Version. Copyright © 1982 by Thomas Nelson, Inc. Used by permission. All rights reserved.

The Internet addresses, email addresses, and phone numbers in this book are accurate at the time of publication. They are provided as a resource. Baker Publishing Group does not endorse them or vouch for their content or permanence.

Cover design by Eric Walljasper

Author is represented by WordServe Literary Group

12 13 14 15 16 17 18   7 6 5 4 3 2 1

In keeping with biblical principles of creation stewardship, Baker Publishing Group advocates the responsible use of our natural resources. As a member of the Green Press Initiative, our company uses recycled paper when possible. The text paper of this book is composed in part of post-consumer waste.

This book would not have happened if it wasn't for the commitment of my editor, Jeff Braun. Thank you, Jeff, for encouraging my voice in this book. Thank you for always being honest to tell me when something "stinks," gentle enough to care if it hurt my feelings, and gracious enough to put up with my whining when it did. As usual, you have gone beyond the call of duty to produce something "edible" for the readers and I am privileged to call you my editor *and* my friend.

Contents

Contents

The Church and the World

About This Book

This is my fourth book. I've been on an amazing journey since writing my first, *Between Heaven and Ground Zero*. And though my life has been filled with many challenges, I've managed to somehow hold on to the hem of Christ's garment and enjoy the most unexpected and glorious ride!

As I've been dragging along on His coattails, I've learned a few things, met a lot of people, and had thousands of dialogues about life. And now Facebook and other social media have made it possible to continue those conversations while I sit in the comfort of my own home. But whether I am face-to-face with people as they bare their soul or I'm reading their "status updates" online, the conversation always comes around to questions about how to live beyond inadequate finances, strained relationships, spiritual obstacles, and other life issues. This book answers some of those questions.

Some of the answers will be easy to swallow, and others, well, not so much. So brace yourself, because as believers in Christ, there comes a time when we must decide: Do we vie for comfort, or do we live outside the box? Do we serve popularity, or do we serve God? Do we tiptoe around the hard stuff with pat answers, or do we dive deeply into the true and uncompromising Word of God?

Life makes no sense outside of the Word of God. And so, this book is filled with God's truth. From beginning to end you will find Bible stories and biblical anecdotes woven together with personal stories to teach us about living above this senseless world.

So as you read, go slow. Pause and reflect, pray, laugh, cry, and embrace the answers you find here. Allow them to move you toward open conversations with God, and then listen. Allow the whispers of God's Holy Spirit to tear down wrong thinking, break old habits, and change your life. Because real transformation is the goal, isn't it?

Now find a comfortable spot in a quiet space, open your heart, and follow me as I follow Christ.

His richest blessings for your life,
Leslie Haskin

Preface

I was a high-spirited, impulsive sixteen-year-old girl. I had a passion for adventure and an insistence on doing things my own way. Add outspoken and rebellious into the mix, and you have a pretty good idea of the Leslie my parents had to deal with in my teenage years.

Particularly challenging for me and for them as well was the summer of 1979. That was the year I lost what I then believed was my most valuable possession. Thankfully, it was also when my father planted a seed that yielded the person I am today.

It was a Friday morning in mid-May and the height of spring fever. Breaking free from the confines of my winter cave in Chicago was all that was on my mind.

The Evergreen Plaza Shopping Mall provided the perfect escape with its annual sidewalk clearance sale. And my high school provided the perfect alibi with cheerleader tryouts taking place immediately after the final bell. I had no business at either event, but I wanted to get to the mall.

I told Dad I would be late coming home. And accompanied by my friend Lora, I left school around noon and headed to the mall. We ran through one store after another like kids in a candy store, sampling all the sales and trying on all the new fashions. Our lunch was a slice of pizza and a shared orange pop. It was great. So great that to this day I still remember how much we laughed.

After a whirlwind of an afternoon, Lora and I headed home at about the time we thought all school activities would be over—4:30 or so.

Taking the city bus seemed like a good idea, and for some reason I decided I would get off the bus near the school and walk my normal route home. Somehow, in my mind, it made my lie to Dad more credible.

As I walked the six blocks to my house, reliving my fabulous day, my thoughts were interrupted by the sound of footsteps fast approaching from behind.

I barely had a chance to turn my head and see who it was when my face met his face. Staring into strange dark eyes and smelling breath harsh with beer, I suddenly felt the nose of a .38-caliber handgun pressed hard into my side. He ordered me into his car, and just like that, my tenacity, high spirit, and love of living ended. I lost my virginity at the hands of a stranger, and my dreams of falling in love and having one special night were lost forever—to the smell of beer breath and cheap cologne.

I spent months in therapy, feeling ashamed, frightened, and very guilty—after all, what happened to me was my fault, right? I mean, if only I'd been where I was supposed to be, and if only I had not lied, and if only, if only, if only. Guilt and depression were killing my spirit.

Then one day Mom and Dad sat me down and gave me a
lesson that today is the gift that keeps on giving. They told
me that love is a gift that must be given freely, and no one
can steal it away from me. They told me that sometimes life
isn't fair, it doesn't make sense, it gives and it takes away. But
through it all, and in all things, we must continue to *know*
that God is always ahead of it . . . no matter what *it* is. Nothing catches Him by surprise, and we can always run into His
arms for comfort. He is the only certainty in life.

My mother pulled my head to her chest, and to this day,
when I stop the noise in my head and slow down to a normal-
life pace, I can remember the sound of her beating heart when
she said, "And this, baby, is the walk of faith."

Today her words make sense. They make life make sense.

My parents were all about perspective and the relevance
of our life experiences. It took me many years to learn that.

This book will walk you through that lesson . . . as I have
lived it and in the ways that I have come to recognize its truth.
In some ways, this book is my parents' gift to the world.

May God be glorified in the work of my hands.

Amen.

Knowing God

"We are in the position of a little child entering a huge library filled with books in many languages. The child knows someone must have written those books. It does not know how. It does not understand the languages in which they are written. The child dimly suspects a mysterious order in the arrangement of the books but doesn't know what it is. That, it seems to me, is the attitude of even the most intelligent human being toward God. We see the universe marvelously arranged and obeying certain laws but only dimly understand these laws. Our limited minds grasp the mysterious force that moves the constellations."

—Albert Einstein

Lord, high and holy, meek and lowly, Thou hast brought me to the valley of vision, where I live in the depths but see Thee in the heights; hemmed in by mountains of sin

I behold Thy glory. Let me learn by paradox that the way down is the way up, that to be low is to be high, that the broken heart is the healed heart, that the contrite spirit is the rejoicing spirit, that the repenting soul is the victorious soul, that to have nothing is to possess all, that to bear the cross is to wear the crown, that to give is to receive, that the valley is the place of vision. Lord, in the daytime stars can be seen from deepest wells, and the deeper the wells the brighter Thy stars shine; let me find Thy light in my darkness, Thy life in my death, Thy joy in my sorrow, Thy grace in my sin, Thy riches in my poverty, Thy glory in my valley.[1]

—"The Valley of Vision," A Puritan Prayer

1

The Question of God

Beyond Ordinary

"I am the Lord, the God of all mankind. Is anything too hard for me?"

—Jeremiah 32:27

Every once in a while, out of the sea of ordinary knowledge, something extraordinary emerges, bringing with it interminable hope and peace that surpasses understanding.

And after thirty-plus years in pursuit of happiness, I am finally satisfied that life and all of its best-kept secrets were revealed in the utterance of a single word: *light*—the natural agent that stimulates sight and makes things visible. And the idea that such complexity can come not only from such simplicity, but out of absolutely nothing, is the most fabulous thing I have ever encountered. With one word, God prescribed the remedy that would heal us on every level of living, unstained or diluted by ambiguity.

Let there be light. Let there be understanding *only* . . . mercy *only* . . . truth *only* . . . healing *only* . . . salvation *only* . . . love *only* . . . hope *only* . . . freedom *only*, and the vastness of other pure cures we have yet to realize we even need. And all of this comes via the grace that came when God said one word: *light*. Light: It's the exposition of any subject or element in order to remove all doubt and uncertainty; surefooted; steadfast; positive.

Almost every story in the Old Testament reveals the nature of a God connected to His people, intervening in ways that always, always, always yield spectacular occurrences.

In Bible times, people who feared God lived in the light. They fasted for weeks at a time and sat for days in praise and wait and wonder of the God who formed the perfect universe by His word. Miracles were commonplace and they expected God to do great things. Life was about God and the connectedness of their lives to Him. The ordinary was illuminated by the extraordinary nature of God, making life a conscious, supernatural experience. Their "every day" included thunderous voices resonating direction from heaven, a talking donkey, a burning bush not consumed, water flowing from rock at a prophet's command, seas divided, and rivers flowing with blood.

There was no ambiguity about who God is—the Alpha, the Omega, the great I AM. Truth indeed was the light, and it resulted in freedom only, deliverance only, and victory only.

But from our modern perspective and by today's standards, their lives were anything but ordinary. Their commonplace is our supernatural. And curiously enough, even though modern living has redefined our relationship with God—and by our actions we have removed Him from His place of wonderment—most of us want and strive for what they had. Though our desire may be to walk in the light, there is a huge gap between what we expect our lives to be and the lives we find ourselves struggling through.

Ah, there's the rub.

Somehow over the years we have stopped living in the mode of giving back to God, and our connection has failed. Our requests of God have become our demands of God, and so our prayers go unanswered. Like the Pharisees, our intellect and our traditions have made "the word of God of none effect" (Mark 7:13 KJV). Consequently, our appreciation for the true nature of God has made small His wonder, and we no longer stand in awe of Him.

How then can we expect great things?

English scientist Aldous Huxley once said, "There was a time when I gazed upon the stars with great wonder and amazement. Now, late in life, I look up at the heavens in the same way in which I gaze upon the faded wallpaper in a railway station waiting room."

Could it be that this is how we look at God? Could it be that modern society and technological advances have turned what once was astonishment over the universe into mere humdrum? Our world is so "smart" that the wonder of God is dumbed down to the point that it can be explained away by another single word: *demystification*. With the simple click of a mouse, we have lost that sheer delight, and the awesomeness of an all-powerful God is forgotten in light of man's capabilities—physical and mental—through the use of technology.

We can extend our brain with computers, our legs with automobiles and airplanes, our eyes with microscopes and telescopes, and even ourselves with the advent of cloning.

As knowledge increases so does agnosticism. The result is a world that is flat and without miracles—predictable, explainable. But the increase of knowledge also increases our need to live beyond the ordinary. And consequently, life doesn't make sense anymore.

I am amazed at how often I hear people attempt to "get" life. They try to take it apart, examine it, and then put it back together again expecting it to work. But how can that be, when in taking it apart we remove the one critical component that makes it all work: light.

Here's an example: If you take a computer apart to see how it works, the first thing you have to do is disconnect it from its power source.

Once disconnected, the first thing you have on your hands is a non-working computer. The second thing you have is a pile of complicated parts that don't work anymore. The third thing you have is a mess that you can't possibly put back together to its maker's specifications and intent because you have no prior understanding of the original design.

Life is like that—complex beyond our vision and comprehension, so much so that the human "self" must be accepted as a mystery known only to God, and life should be accepted as a gift from Him as well, incapable of being understood by mere mortals. Think about it, if God created life, and that includes us, do we really think our brain is equally matched to His so that we can understand all of it?

What we are able to know is that life is God-given: intricate yet simple, brief yet everlasting, glorious yet sorrowful. And when complete and put together, it is awesome and it works. But when in our search for knowledge and control beyond what God has provided we tear life apart, it breaks down.

There is nothing wrong with our quest for knowledge. In fact, it is natural to crave understanding and then to grow in that understanding (Proverbs 4:7). But there is a thin line between the quest for knowledge and the quest for "god-dom," which is more than the desire to know; it is a desire to know what only God knows. This is the prideful self-interest that draws the mind up to something higher, purer, and loftier than it is capable of. And if I recall, it was that kind of desire that disconnected us from the power source and complicated life in the first place.

Reflection—Beyond Ordinary

Politeness is sometimes mistaken for reverence, irreverence for informality, and calling ourselves "unworthy of God" for humility. True respect and sincere humility bloom when there is a sense of who God is and of His presence. There is nothing *ordinary* about God, so every step in our journey of getting to know Him should be and will be extraordinary. Pause here and reflect on who God is to you. Do you see Him as God or simply as superhuman?

An Offered Prayer

Lord,

Will you show yourself to me in the degree I can bear it? I know that seeing you will grip me and stir me with your holiness, and I will begin to realize the authority you have in my life and in the world. Strip me, Father, of my "ordinary view." Amen.

2

Why Is Life So Complicated?

Once Upon a Time in the Garden

"Do not conform to the pattern of this world, but be transformed by the renewing of your mind. Then you will be able to test and approve what God's will is—his good, pleasing and perfect will."

—Romans 12:2

In the beginning, God created heaven and earth. He formed Adam from dirt and Eve from Adam's rib (a point we'll discuss later in the book). Life was great.

Adam was purposed by God to control all of creation. Eve supported Adam, and together they would "be fruitful, multiply, and fill the earth." It was a peaceful and simple existence. They enjoyed a perfect relationship with each other, the world around them, and with God. They lived in the light.

I imagine their world as breathtaking, a never-ending landscape of flowers, mountains, valleys, and immeasurable bodies of water. Every plant and tree, with the exception of two—the Tree of Life and the Tree of Knowledge of Good and Evil—were provided for their food. Their bodies were healthy and strong.

I imagine the animals roaming freely about, talking to Adam and Eve and resting beneath tall trees. The sound of singing birds and a soft fragrance of lavender was constant in the air, creating an ambiance of tranquility.

The streets were sprinkled with gold, and precious stones had been tossed here and there by God's own hand (Genesis 2:11–12). Both large and small rocks, strategically placed beneath the peaks of the waters, created the cascades and falls where God himself walked. It was majestic.

One day Adam and Eve were out for their early evening stroll. Perhaps they were holding hands in that relaxed manner couples do. Eve likely talked about everything that had happened that day, and Adam more than likely pretended to listen.

Now, the serpent, who had visited them on more than one occasion, came into the garden again to tempt Adam to call God a liar. But Adam ignored the creature and kept walking. Eve, on the other hand, was intrigued.

They walked and talked together until they came to their favorite place in the garden where the path to the Tree of Life met with the garden's cascading waters. The lions often fed there. The Tree of Knowledge of Good and Evil was close by. It was there at the base of that tree that a couple of larger stones provided ample room to rest and to sit in awe of the God who formed the perfect universe with the utterance of a single word. The vastness of the earth came to the fore there, as they gazed out into the skies. *What a glorious day,* Eve thought to herself.

As the sun began to set, clearly defined bands of color lifted from the waters and shimmered across its glass-like surface and through the atmosphere. A flash of blue and green lit the waters while soft winds pushed surface water away from the shore, allowing bottom waters to rise and kiss the rocks. The last of the sun's orange rays slid through the trees and made them even more alluring. It was perfect.

Adam lay back and praised God. Eve also reclined, and in the final minutes of the setting sun, its light shone through the trees and caused her eyes to rest on its fruit.

The serpent appeared.

Now, the serpent was craftier than the other animals that God had made. It drew closer to the woman and whispered to her: "Did God really say, 'You must not eat from any tree in the garden'?"

At this point, being a woman myself, I imagine Eve replayed every conversation she ever had with God in her head, searching for a loophole that would give her an out. And when she couldn't find one, she simply did what most of us do; she left out the things that didn't serve her own purpose.

She looked at the serpent and said, "God said we may eat fruit from the trees in the garden, but not from the tree in the middle." I imagine Adam nudged her to remind her of all that God said. She quickly added, "Not to even touch it, or we will die."

The serpent twisted his face in response and shook his head to imply disbelief. "You will not certainly die," he said to Eve. "God just knows that when you eat from that particular tree, your eyes will be opened, and you will know all that He knows."

Well, that was all Eve needed to hear. Her mind raced. She quickly rationalized what the serpent was saying and thought, *Surely God would not plant a tree that would kill us.*

The serpent nodded to egg her on. Now convinced, Eve smiled, took the fruit, ate it, and then turned to Adam, who was still with her, and he ate too. Somewhere in the distance a wolf howled.

Night had fallen.

I don't imagine it took very long for the garden's splendor to change. The brilliance of colors began to fade from the earth. Large bodies of water receded. The intensity of the sun lost its glow, and bird songs were less inspired.

Adam and Eve's eyes began to be opened. They saw their dying world. They were naked and ashamed.

As the serpent watched, his grin turned to laughter when, under the shadow of night, Adam and Eve ran about the garden frantically gathering fig leaves and sewing them together to hide themselves.

By dawn they could hear God walking in the garden. And likely feeling guilty about what they had done, they hid behind a tree. Then God called to Adam, "Where are you?"

The trees whistled and waved in the breeze of God's breath. Adam responded. "I heard you in the garden. But I was afraid because I was naked. So I hid."

Now the serpent, knowing he had destroyed the pure relationship God had with man, drew closer to Adam to hear. God asked, "Who told you that you were naked? Did you eat from the tree that I commanded you not to eat from?" Adam lowered his head. "The woman you put here with me—she gave me some fruit from the tree and I ate it."

God looked at Eve. "What is this you have done?"

And with that, the simplicity of life was gone. Our lives since then have been lived out in answer to that one question. Indeed, what had she done?

I've heard this story told many times—each time with an emphasis on the first sin: Adam and Eve's disobedience to the commandment of God. But I think there was a lot more going on there.

While man's most obvious sin was disobedience, the disobedience was only evidence of his unbelief. And in the same way, his obedience would have been evidence of faith. If Eve really trusted God, she would not have fallen victim to deception and God's word would have been enough. Knowing who had forbidden the fruit, not why the fruit was forbidden, trusting what God said, and not needing to understand why he said it, should have been enough. *"And that, baby, is the walk of faith."* That's good fruit.

God desires that we bear good fruit based not on our understanding of *why* we are to do as He requires, but simply that He requires it.

I don't know about you, but growing up, my siblings and I were not even allowed to *ask* my parents why. If Mom or Dad told us *no,* then no it was—plain and simply "'Cause I said so." No questions asked. So if that is the expectation of our human parents, why should we expect any less from God? Should it be any less? What does it matter why He placed the tree there? This is God we're talking about, and He can do whatever He wants just because He said so.

But like Eve, our obedience to God is often conditional. We want to understand *why* we should obey God before we obey Him. We want to understand why God has commanded some things and prohibited others. We want Him to justify His edicts. And when we don't understand the reasons, we often reject the instructions.

With that said, let's look at the not-so-obvious sin. I believe that even though Adam and Eve's sin looked the same from the outside, their transgressions were as different as life and death. The Bible tells us that even though the first person to actually disobey God's commandment not to eat of the tree was the woman, sin entered the world through one "man" (Romans 5:12). First Timothy 2:14 says, "Adam was not the one deceived; it was the woman who was deceived and became a sinner." In other words, Eve broke the rules because she was deceived, but Adam broke the rules knowing full well what he was doing!

He sat there with Eve and allowed the serpent to deceive her, knowing exactly what the consequences would be. And with that same knowing, Adam ate the fruit as well. Adam knowingly chose death over life. Why? There had to be some motivation. There had to be some hidden desire in Adam that compelled him to *give* the enemy place and *disobey* God.

I submit to you that Adam's motivation was the same motivation that compels us to sin against God today. It was and is our self-serving interest, pride, and a desire to be something we were never meant to be—God. Taking the forbidden fruit revealed the condition of Adam's heart, but his heart was already corrupt.

Many of us live this way today. But instead of fruit, we take for ourselves possessions: more things, more friends, more memberships, more groups, and more fame. Instead of being passively deceived, we instigate it.

Like Adam, our hearts are steeped in arrogance and self-importance, shrouded by breaches that on the surface are disobedience and a belief that God is withholding something good from us. But on a deeper level it is our own self-importance and pride. At the heart of our transgression is the longing to be equal with God and share in His power and glory.

We have disconnected from the power source, disassembled our lives, and removed all the parts that make life work. Consequently, our ability to sense God has disintegrated and we have replaced Him with human explanations and intellect. We have become the center of our universe, calling God a liar and questioning everything that doesn't fit in our apple cart. If some thing or some idea doesn't make sense to us, we simply reject it. The Greeks call it *hubris*. Christ calls it *sin*. And today, we simply call it *complicated*.

Whatever you label it, the bottom line is that we live in a fallen world. We have allowed the devil to complicate every level of our living. The world as we know it continues to fall apart, and it looks less and less like the garden of God's original intent. On a global scale, the devil has corrupted government and spread religious-based terrorism throughout the nations. Nationally, he has polluted our neighborhoods with violence, disrupted families, seduced our children with addictions, and bound parents in depression, anxiety, and a host of other sicknesses that have thrown us into such despair that we don't see God anymore.

So many people have become weary of trusting God. Delayed answers to prayers have caused a loss of hope. But even though we are in the world, we are not of the world (John 17:14–15). We were created by God to commune with God.

And if we remain disconnected from Him, if we continue to desire to know all that He knows, if we trust outside voices more than we trust the voice of God, then our lives will never work and they will never make sense. That's it, plain and simple.

You see, sin complicates even the simplest things. Molehills become mountains. And even the best laid plans will fail.

The answer lies in how we trust God in every situation. Through it all, He is our redeemer. If we give ourselves over to Him completely, if we obey His words and leave the consequences to Him, our lives will become the extraordinary lives they were intended to be. We move mountains. We conquer giants. We live connected, uncomplicated, and complete.

Reflection—God's Intent

As believers, it ought to be said of us, what you see is what you get! No duplicity, just naked honesty—even at times when it might be painfully exposing. We should live lives of transparency. Like Adam and Eve, what sins in your life are you trying to hide from God?

An Offered Prayer

Lord,

You know that in certain situations with certain people I find it so easy to pretend. Help me to stop hiding my true feelings and to live with a heart that is revealed. In Jesus' name. Amen.

3

How Do I Hear From You, God, in the Middle of the Chaos?

ROFL, I Think the Holy Spirit Just Texted Me

"Speak, for your servant is listening."

—1 Samuel 3:10

This is no anomaly. Our creation right is to live in the light and to be in constant communion with God—and not only in prayer or occasional fellowship. Communion goes much deeper than that—to that place in us where we are linked to God and His ways are familiar. His voice is known. His presence is perceived, and we follow after Him.

Before their transgression, Adam and Eve knew God in that way. They enjoyed a connectedness with Him that transcended words. The Bible bears witness to this.

In the third chapter of Genesis (v. 8 KJV), we read that Adam "heard the voice of the Lord God walking in the garden in the cool of the day." So in his faultless form and by design, Adam recognized God on all sensory levels—simultaneously. His consciousness of God's presence together with his experience of God's ways opened him up to more than the mere sensation of God as an external entity. He perceived Him inwardly as well. Adam heard, felt, smelled, saw, and sensed God's *Ruah*—His spirit, breath, voice, wind—moving, stirring, creating, and walking, all at once.

It stands to reason. Because in no way can the infinite God—who by saying a word caused nothing to become something, chaos to become order, darkness to become light—be limited by mortal observation. He is not reduced to the size that we can understand Him simply because we do not have the capacity to fully understand Him.

Yet I have no doubt that if we would live as we were designed to live, His presence would stir us in the same way it stirred Adam. That's *knowing* God. And knowing Him only comes through constant communion and communication with Him. The more we commune with Him, the easier it will be to hear Him through whatever means He chooses.

God revealed himself to men in the Old Testament in dreams, visions, experiences, symbols, and many other ways. He spoke to Moses through a burning bush, to Balaam through a donkey, to Samuel in a loud, audible voice, and to Israel through a cloud by day and a pillar of fire by night (Exodus 13:21–22). The New Testament shows Him speaking to John the Baptist through a dove and to Paul on the road to Damascus.

Hebrews 1:1–3 (KJV) says, "God, who at sundry times and in divers manners spake in time past unto the fathers by the prophets, hath in these last days spoken unto us by his Son." In other words, God is and always has been articulate in His universe.

So why do we think He doesn't speak to us today? Why does it seem that the lines of communication have been closed to us?

Personally, I don't believe that God, who throughout the generations spoke so boldly to His children, would suddenly lapse into silence or that communion with Him would become something we have to conjure up or imagine. So the question is not why God doesn't speak to us today, but rather why we don't hear Him.

I know from my own experiences that hearing God is not a matter for the faint of heart. It takes time to know Him and become proficient in His ways. Hearing God demands that our full attention be given to everything going on in and around us at the same time. We must open ourselves up to the experience of sensory overload . . . like hearing God's voice walking.

The reality of life is that spirit is the source of all that exists. Matter interacts with sound, interacts with feeling, interacts with spirit, and God is spirit (John 4:24). So even though we are not aware of it, God connects and communicates on every level of His creation, just as He always has. Our forefathers knew that about Him. They expected it from Him, so they listened and watched for Him in all things.

For example, I know my son, Eliot, and he knows me. We are constantly communicating with one another. I watch his body language, his gestures, his facial expressions, and his behavior in order to fully "hear" him. And I do. I know, for example, that when his eyes jump during our conversation, he's not being completely honest. I know that when his chest heaves, he's angry. His eyes well up when he's touched by something, he cleans when he's stressed, and when he sleeps a lot, it means he's depressed or avoiding something.

And it works both ways. My responses to him are as important as his "communications" to me. I know when to back off, when to offer my shoulder, when to unassumingly make recommendations that he pursue a certain action, and I know when to push. I know when to just listen and when to press in. I know what he will do and what he won't do in just about every situation, and he knows the same of me.

Over the years, we've learned how to listen and hear each other without needing words. We've exposed to each other the innermost parts of our souls. And by doing so we've gained the kind of intimacy and vulnerability that hearing *and* being heard requires. My son and I are connected.

God desires no less a connection with His children, and hearing Him demands it.

So I've been thinking a lot lately about how we connect to God and our capacity to hear Him. I wonder if the static noise and immediacy of our culture, along with the ubiquity of technology, specifically the Internet, has become so loud that we have become blind *and* deaf to God's voice; so unaffected by its indescribable and evidential excellence that much lesser things excite us and take up our time.

In fact, time-displacement theory suggests that if we start a new activity or begin to use a new technology, we will have to quit or reduce the time we spend with former activities. (Hmm . . . pause and reflect.) So even though there is no denying the good that the Internet has placed at our fingertips, I wonder if it has nudged God out of the already inadequate time we set aside for Him each day.

Please don't misunderstand me. We all have busy lives. But consider a relationship or marriage in which the couple spends just an hour (or less) a day with each other. What can they accomplish in so little time? How much intimacy can be achieved? How do they really get to know each other and learn to communicate? Further complicating things is our easy access and over usage of ready online devices. Between texting and tweeting, the vulnerability and honesty of conversation that real communication demands is lost to the quickness of the keypad or keyboard.

The rapid pace of online communication allows little time for contemplation or action. And we adjust to that. It becomes our norm, and the usual old standards of communicating become substandard.

I know I am guilty of making the compromise. I've adjusted my behavior to fit the instant-response culture of the Internet, and honestly, I'm not so sure I like what I see. The ways I'm speaking and writing lately are not a true representation of the real me.

You see, I'm very cerebral, contemplative, and deliberate in my conversations. I like getting to know the mind and thought patterns of the person I'm speaking with; I like going deep. But in the immediacy of the World Wide Web, there is no time for reflection, no time to consider, and certainly no time to "know" anyone.

Take Facebook, for example. If I don't respond right away to a status or post or discussion, it moves on without me. If I take the time to consider my response, by the time I'm ready to add any value, my position is no longer relevant. And it's the same way with cell phones. More and more people would rather text than talk. Slow, measured, considered communication is a thing of the past. Everything is coded text language. And not only do you have to text, you have to be quick about it.

So despite my resistance, if I want to "talk" more with Eliot and his sister, Monai, I have to speak the language of texting and get those thumbs moving. ROFL.

One night I was talking on the phone to a friend about hearing God. In fact, we were discussing this very chapter. We talked and shared Scripture for a little more than an hour, so that by the time the conversation was finished, I was feeling particularly spiritual and in perfect communion with God.

I put my phone down next to the sofa and turned on the TV to CBN. No more than two minutes passed and my phone buzzed. It was a text message from Eliot.

> Eliot: prolly b omw in hr . . . want somthin
> Me: Nope. Thanks.
> Eliot: k
> Me: What time do you think you'll be home?
> Eliot: idk . . . ilu . . . gnite
> Me: ?
> Eliot:
> Me: what time is idk . . . ilu . . . gnite?
> Eliot:
> Me: Eliot!!!
> Eliot:

I waited for his response but nothing came. It took only seconds for my messed up, 9/11-ridden mother's mind to go "there." *Oh, no, he must have been texting while driving! Oh, Lord, my son is in a ditch!* What else could it be? For me, there was no other reason that he would suddenly stop texting in the middle of our conversation.

Panicked but feeling residual bits of the "speak to it" spirituality left in me, I started praying. I rebuked the devil. I took dominion. I decreed, declared, and shouted every other religious *d* word I could think of. Then, finally, after what seemed like forever, and just as the growing mountain of anxiety approached insurmountable, my phone buzzed. I ran and picked it up, It read: "EL ROI."

I dialed Monai, and to my surprise, she answered.

> Monai: Yep?
> Me: I haven't heard from your brother in almost an hour.
> Monai: Okay?
> Me: He just stopped texting me in the middle of a text. What does "idk . . . ilu . . . gnite" mean?
> Monai: I don't know. I love you. Good night.
> Me: Oh, you busy? Just tell me real quick what it means.

Monai, now laughing hysterically, said, "I just did. It means 'I don't know. I love you. Good night.'"

Then after she composed herself and told me how old I am, she went on to assure me that knowing Eliot, if he didn't answer, it was because he'd probably ("prolly") lost power to his phone. "Everybody's not falling in ditches, you know," she said.

"Okay, then, Ms. Smarty," I said, "What does EL ROI mean?"

Her voice faded to background and I heard her saying "idk" just as Eliot walked through the front door. Before I could say a word to him, he told me his phone had died.

"Did you text me again?" he asked.

"Yes. And what does EL ROI mean?"

He laughed. "I have no idea. I never texted that."

———

In our present society, the quick pace, constant movement, and swarm of activity make it hard enough to communicate with people we see every day. How can we expect it to slow down enough for us to communicate with a God we do not see? Except in fully *knowing* Him (we'll get more into the *knowing* in a later chapter) can we expect to hear Him even in things that happen around us every day.

Monai had to remind me about who Eliot is in order to reassure me that his communication was not interrupted by driving into a dreaded ditch. To know Eliot is to also know that his awareness of and sensitivity to my concerns (and fear of ditches) would compel him to complete his text—even if it meant doing so *from* a ditch.

God is faithful like that, and even more so. To know Him is to know that about Him. He is the same God today that He was yesterday, and He will remain unchanged tomorrow and forever. He is still very articulate in His universe.

God speaks. The onus is on us to press in and quiet the noise of everyday distractions so that we become better acquainted with His actions, His ways, how the world responds to Him, His Word, and His voice (John 10:27). We must be willing to discontinue the Pharisee-like behavior; exchange our television and Internet time, our small groups and fellowship dinners, even our ministries, charities, and daily devotions if they are driven by our response to the world and not our response to God.

God wants our honest heart. He wants us to pray when we feel Him tugging at us, pick up our Bible when we hear Him calling to us, and tarry with Him when we feel Him near.

God wants more than just noise and words of worship. He wants a lifestyle that takes us outside of ourselves and lends itself to prayer in prostration and hours on bended knee. No ritual or tradition takes us outside of ourselves and puts us in a place of deeper communion with God. None of them teaches us that God is speaking in the continuous present. And we will never see it that way or hear His voice walking until we allow our minds to be directed toward living in purposeful pursuit of relationship with God that hears Him speak in and through all of His creation . . . even the technological ones . . . *lol.*

Weeks after my texting fiasco with Eliot and Monai, I was sitting alone in my family room, studying the names of God and committing them to memory. I came to *EL ROI.* It means "the God who sees." I was floored.

Once again, God is truly amazing! More and more over the years I'm finding that I'm less and less surprised by the many ways God chooses to speak to me. But I'm always so very let down at how long it takes for me to hear Him. You see, in the middle of the panic and chaos of trying to decode the hip new text language that Eliot and Monai use, I had totally missed what God was saying in His text. God saw Eliot, and He knew where he was! EL ROI.

God sees us wherever we are. Spiritually and physically, He well knows too what we need every minute of every hour of every day—even if we need, by any means necessary, to hear His still, small voice of assurance.

I think in the long run, when we step outside the conventional talking heads and look to hear God in less traditional ways, we'll find Him. Mountains will move, thunder will roll for us, seas will open up, donkeys will speak, and text messages will come through loud and clear.

After I read EL ROI in the list of names for God, I ran to my phone praising that name and needing to spread the joy. I picked up my little texting device, which surprisingly found nimble thumbs sliding across its little keypad as I sent a message to Eliot: "ROFL, I think the Holy Spirit texted me."

Reflection—The Language of the Master

The most effective communicators are *always* the best listeners. Jesus demonstrated how to hear from God and how prayer isn't just talking to God when we want something from Him. Prayer is a way of life, whereby we express communion with the Father through listening first. In listening to God, how have you limited God in the ways He speaks to you?

An Offered Prayer

Father,

You are the Great Communicator, and I desire to hear from you. Speak, Holy Spirit of God. I am listening. Amen.

4

God, Where Are You?

GPS, Expedia, and Google Maps

"You will seek me and find me when you seek me with all your heart."

—Jeremiah 29:13

Meeting God turns out to be nothing like just hearing about Him.

And these days I'm constantly listening in order to "see" God . . . like His voice walking in plain sight. I'm hearing Him, and I'm finding that even in the simplest things, He is original, complex, and beautiful. And His voice, clearly constant and articulate in His universe, can be heard by whatever means available, provided we settle ourselves to hear.

I'm settling.

As I'm writing this chapter, I'm shoveling a slice of Chicago-style pizza down my throat in one of those ambiance-filled New York pizza joints, where the seating is ample in oversized wooden benches heavily carved with the signatures of those who came before me. The smoky flavor of burned crust is in the air, the lighting is dim, and the sounds of conversations going on around me swirl about my head and put me in a great mood. Sure it's a little cheesy, but it's just the way I like it; deep dish, savory, so hot it stops just shy of burning my mouth with cheese so thick that when I pull it away from my teeth, it stretches out for days. Yummy.

A few months ago, I had the tasty pleasure of having this very same kind of pizza with a few old friends at the restaurant chain's downtown Chicago location. The seating there was outside bistro-type tables, poorly positioned and crowded by passersby who repeatedly bumped the back of my too-narrow chair and interrupted the flow of a conversation that was much too deep to enjoy over pizza anyway.

I hate cold pizza.

We talked about present-day health issues and the economy. This evolved into world economics, which turned into, you guessed it, global despondency and how for so many, God seems absent from it all. Quite a mouthful.

At times our voices stopped just shy of a fevered pitch on hot topics like global terrorism, natural disasters, and religious differences. Questions kept surfacing around whether or not we are living in the last days and end-times prophesies are being fulfilled, how we should pray, and where God is right now.

Normally, I'm a backseat kind of person when it comes to conversations like those. I don't like where they can lead:

public displays and emotional prayers. It's not appetizing at all.

But I had a point. What if God is choosing not to be found in this present darkness? What if, instead of meeting us in our chaos, He is intentionally staying distant in order to draw us out of it? Call me crazy, but do we really expect to find a God of perfect peace and order in the middle of confusion and chaos?

The truth is, we have created for ourselves shockingly dysfunctional lives, and they have become our norm. We are comfortable, and changing anything about our lifestyles is just too hard. We complain about our relationships that don't work, yet we repeat bad behaviors time and again that keep creating relationships that don't work. We pray about our finances, yet we continue to overspend. We cry and seek God's face for deliverance from our addictions and depression, but we won't fast or pray or receive our deliverance. Let's be candid. Most of us have prayed with someone and shared with them biblical solutions for their problems, but rather than working to fix the problem, they come back with reasons the situation remains the same.

By our own choices, we have distanced ourselves from our Father God, and the enemy of this world has blinded our eyes to His presence (2 Corinthians 4:4). We continue to live in darkness.

Behavioral experts say people who have been set free from difficult situations don't always embrace freedom as we might expect. They are often drawn back to what is more familiar to them. The trauma and hardship and a life of struggle become their norm. Clinically speaking, dysfunction attracts dysfunction. So instead of turning their backs on the anguish and saying no to it, they feel more comfortable with the familiar and return to that "safe" place that only breeds sorrow and pain.

But what we don't realize is the fact that our personal dysfunction becomes our nation's dysfunction becomes a fallen world, and we will never find God in dysfunction, period. He will not be found living among the dead. Light has no place in the darkness. Second Corinthians 6:14 asks us, "What fellowship can light have with darkness?"

In every deliverance story I've read in which the presence of God was known and felt and realized, God commanded His people to first "leave this place or that place" or "come out from that place or this place," and "then I will" do something or another. God is always "calling a people out of a people." He does not join us in the confusion. For God is not a God whose ways are without order, but a God of peace.

In 1 Corinthians 6:17–18, Paul wrote, "Come out from among them, and be ye separate, saith the Lord, and touch not the unclean thing; and I will receive you. And will be a Father unto you, and ye shall be my sons and daughters, saith the Lord Almighty" (KJV). In Revelation, John heard a voice from heaven calling God's people out of Babylon (18:4). In biblical terms, *Babylon* means "confusion." Noah was called out of an evil world by God, Abraham left a country of idolaters to seek out a city "whose builder and maker is God," and Jesus called His disciples out of a system of worship that had been perverted by the ignorance, carnality, and traditions of its religious leaders.

In our generation, God is once again calling true believers out of the chaos of this world and unto himself (Isaiah 41:9). If you want peace and order in your life, you *must* hear and answer the call of God to come out from the dysfunction of it. Why seek healing from cancer and continue to smoke?

I believe God's desire is that we leave the familiar ways of disorder in favor of living soberly and aware in His presence. I believe He wants us to encounter Him. From the simplicity of blowing winds and intricacies of flower petals to the thundering voice that comes from the cloud and falling towers, God is available for daily contact.

And these encounters, big and small, bring healing and transformation to our lives. They open wide our chests and expose our whole hearts to the One who created them in the first place. And behold, old things pass away and all things become new. Amen!

On the day of Pentecost, God went to extremes to make himself known to the people. He still does today. He welcomes encounters with every person who opens his or her heart to Him. He extends an open invitation, not some cheap vendor agreement or an indulgence for continued self-aggrandizement. The God of Israel is calling His people out to something much better. And He is readily accessible to those who are willing to make Him Lord of their lives and enter into relationship with Him.

People down through time have been saved from spiritual death the same way. They come out of their individual darkness and into God's salvation by grace through faith in the atoning blood of Jesus. Then His Holy Spirit meets them there and baptizes them in power and strength. From that day on, we read of their more-than-incredible encounters with God and the miraculous.

But here's the rub: We won't get the big thunderous encounters with Him (the open visions, the angelic visitations,

being caught up into heaven) until we are every-time respon-
sive to Him in the commonplace of our lives. We must first
train our eyes and ears to behold Him in situations as ef-
fortless as having a good gut laugh at a child blowing milk
from his nose after you've felt depressed all day, or seeing a
commercial on television that addresses the very thing you've
been questioning all week, or driving a nail through a fresh
piece of wood and seeing the sap flow red.

If we reprogram our internal GPS systems to look outside the usual neighborhoods and broaden the scope of our
Google maps to search from a higher perspective, we'll find
God. After that, it's a cakewalk. Well, not exactly, but the
world will become less painful living with Him in view.

So where is God? A. W. Tozer said, "Start the day seeking
God's presence and search for Him all through the day and
revel in the gracious encounters of God throughout the day."

Nice. The awareness of Him is all around us and His presence is with everyone who seeks Him. Our mission to perceive
Him begins the minute we pick up the Bible. Because it is in
reading it that our spirit is quickened and the God of the Bible
leaps from its pages, breaks into our day, and shows himself
to us through work, at the hospital, in the classroom, on the
street, through a homeless man, a walk in the park, even in
dreams. Glory to God! He is alive!

We taste of Him and our appetite for Him is increased. We
long for more of Him and we begin looking intently at the
world we live in, on the hunt to see what a living and powerful
God can show us in all of life, because we know that He can be
found in all of life. Hmm, yes, God can be found in all of life.

So as I reflect more, perhaps our limited view of Him is
simply due to poor positioning. Maybe we have just gotten

too comfortable to "turn" from our crowded dysfunctional lives. Maybe it's easier to keep indulging in conversations that are hard to digest and being carried away in cheesy situations that prevent us from really enjoying the abundance of life that God is calling us to.

And so perhaps in the persistence of His love, just maybe, like those huge benches in that New York pizza place, God carves evidence of His presence in the most visible and obscure places and then gives us plenty of room to take notice. It's up to us to take notice.

Reflection—Finding God in an Encounter With Him

Jeremiah 29:13 says, "You will seek me and find me when you seek me with all your heart." We find God through our encounters with Him. History demonstrates that in order for us to be aware of God's presence in our lives on a daily basis, each generation needs its own encounter or great awakening with Him on national and personal levels. Think back and reflect on your supernatural encounters with God and His Holy Spirit—knee-weakening moments like they had at Pentecost. If you have not had one, perhaps the time has come.

An Offered Prayer

Holy Spirit of God,

I want to be filled with you and not resist you. I am longing to experience your presence and to have an encounter with you that changes me and helps me to live from the inside out. Fill me. Change me. Mold me in the perfect image of your living Son, Jesus Christ. Amen.

5

How Can I Read Your Word and Still Not Find Help?

KJV, NKJV, and NIV...
It's All Greek to Me

"Study to shew thyself approved unto God, a workman that needeth not to be ashamed, rightly dividing the word of truth."

—2 Timothy 2:15 KJV

S o now we focus on going hard after God—the essence of knowing Him. This is far more than just a gathering of facts and information about Him and much more than a list of character traits and deeds. Going hard after God gives us insight into His divine nature, and the quest begins beneath the surface of His biblical Word.

Quite simply, this means that our time with God will be spent in prayer and listening and in-depth Bible study with a goal to know the God who is revealed through its pages. In doing so, we can better apply what we know to our lives.

The Bible is filled with all kinds of wonderful and practical advice on every subject that will ever come up on our Christian journey, giving us great insights into the nature of God, ourselves, and the world.

And today, when false doctrine and lies are being spread like butter, it's critical that we read and understand God's Word for ourselves.

Most Christians today don't spend time in the Word or form their own biblical views. They inherit them either from their family teaching or from the doctrine of the church they attend. So when they first start reading the Bible independently, they are either just memorizing Scripture, expecting certain verses will magically change their lives, or they're reading the Bible like it's an almanac, searching for facts and chronology.

Hundreds of Bible-study tools support methods like those, suggesting that we memorize and pray the Bible back to God. There are even tools to help us "get through it" in a year. But all things considered, I think those are "Bible-light" approaches, and I'm not convinced of their value. It's not to say our hearts are in the wrong place; it's our practice. Even though the Bible *will* always bring life no matter the approach, if we want more from the Word, we have to put more into it.

To focus only on isolated passages and take them out of context risks seriously distorting the meaning of Scripture, and we lose sight of the person of God. To read by timeline is a cursory glance at truth and will not teach us how to discern the word of truth, leaving us deceived and believing things that promote a system of understanding that has an appearance of the gospel, but is actually anti-gospel (2 Corinthians 11:4; Galatians 1:6). And if we continue to treat the Bible like an almanac and read by the calendar, putting our spiritual lives on the "hobby" level, God is not indifferent. We'll get out of it what we put into it, even if that is only half the truth.

I remember having a few doctrinal conversations about something in the Bible that at first glance appeared to be inconsistent. I had to finally just say to the person, "Yes, I know that's what it seems, but there is a whole lot more to it than just that."

The Holy Bible is not just a book of related facts. Beneath its surface is a wealth of information so intricate, so consistent, and so flawlessly tied in with prophecy and foreshadowing that to try to take it in by memorizing a Scripture here and a Scripture there or reading through it in a hurried one year will cause you to lose the depth of it.

By design, it is better read as one perfect story. So while taking it in with big gulps will choke you to death, slow and purposeful reading is absorbed into your core. That's the only way to really *get* it. Joshua 1:8 tells us, "Keep this Book of the Law always on your lips; meditate on it day and night, so that you may be careful to do everything written in it. Then you will be prosperous and successful."

When I was a little girl, I remember the older people in the church used to refer to the Bible as the Good Book. They believed it was and still is today all good, God-breathed so life inheres in it. It is perfectly written, so meaning permeates it, authority for living is revealed through its pages, and the power of life and death are built into it. No matter how you read it, it's all God. No other book reveals Him so vividly. Like an open diary, we read about the things He did for His people, what moves His heart, what grieves His spirit, and why He is so mindful of us.

And so the purpose of reading it is not only to know the laws of God, but to know God. Our objective in committing it to memory should not be to bring our lives in line with some code of conduct. Instead, we should be carefully observing and taking aim at the characteristics of God, modeling ourselves to live in His image and be transformed through the power of its influence—seeing Him and wanting to be like Him . . . a personal God, not a list of facts, virtues, or moral maxims.

You see, qualities and virtues don't save people, God does. They don't hear prayers, feel compassion, or show mercy. They don't die on a cross and redeem mankind from sin and trouble; God did that and we in return love and worship Him for what He has done.

And this takes time. Knowing God is a lifetime process of intimacy through hearing and observing and challenging ourselves beyond the acceptable norm.

Using Bible-study aids is cool, but with something so critical to life, we shouldn't risk relying *solely* on someone else's study of God's Word to reveal God to us. Knowing Him is individual. The Word tells us to study for ourselves and know God (2 Timothy 2:15).

One of my absolute favorite theologians, A. W. Tozer, expressed this opinion beautifully in his book *The Pursuit of God*:

How tragic that we in this dark day have had our seeking done for us by our teachers. Everything is made to center upon the initial act of "accepting" Christ . . . and we are not expected thereafter to crave any further revelation of God to our souls. We have been snared in the coils of a spurious logic, which insists that if we have found him we need no more seek him. This is set before us as the last word in orthodoxy, and it is taken for granted that no Bible-taught Christian ever believed otherwise. Thus the whole testimony of the worshiping, seeking, singing Church on that subject is crisply set aside. The experimental heart-theology of a grand army of fragrant saints is rejected in favor of a smug interpretation of Scripture, which would certainly have sounded strange to an Augustine, a Rutherford, or a Brainerd.[1]

Simpler said, reading and understanding the Bible is a personal pursuit. We have to do it for ourselves in order for the truth of it to become alive in us. It is so rich and so personal that it speaks to each of us individually, exactly where we need it.

Years ago, when I gave my whole self to the Lord God, I started reading the Bible to learn what I should and shouldn't be doing in order to live a good Christian life. I was gathering the facts and memorizing Scripture, as I was taught. Honestly, it was a bit of a challenge for me to really understand what I was reading. It all seemed disjointed. The *thee*s and *thou*s threw me off, and honestly, I struggled quite a bit.

At that time, my son was in a Christian school, and he knew all about the Old Testament. He loved it. He also memorized the entire book of Revelation and recorded every proverb on audiotape. Eliot kept telling me about stories that he'd read that he thought were somehow similar to our lives. I thought, *Great. Thanks, Eliot.*

Well, one day over a macaroni and cheese dinner, he told me that except for the fact that I was single, I was "just like that woman in the Bible named Deborah who led an army of God to victory." My reaction to what I'm sure he believed was a relatively innocuous comment threw me for a loop. *Really?!* I had no idea who she was, so I searched for her and found her in Judges 4–5. And do you know what? Eliot was right. Deborah and I did share similar gifts, including our drive and desire to please God. I was so intrigued that I kept searching for more people, more stories, and more situations like mine.

What I found was more stories, more people, more situations like mine and a very visible God, interactive and ever-present in their lives. I saw myself in the quiet reflection and questioning spirit of Paul, the opinionated stubbornness of Jonah, the broken heart for people yet reluctance to go it alone of Jeremiah, and even the forthcoming and somewhat brash preaching style of John the Baptist (see Mark 1) was familiar to me.

In every situation, God was right there, loving and guiding that person according to his or her specific needs and His riches in glory. Amen!!

And the more I read, the more I saw a unique and personal God dealing with everyday people and situations just like my own. And I liked Him. The more I liked Him, the more deeply in love with Him I became. And from those days onward, all I ever wanted to be was like Him. It was like reading God's journal. And for the first time in my life I got up close and inside of Him, and He in me—a real progressive revelation of who He really is came to me. And knowing God turns out to be nothing like just hearing about Him.

We can sit in any church or classroom and hear enough about mourning that we understand what it means and what it's all about. But when we are weeping at the grave of someone we love, it takes on a whole new dimension of understanding. We then *know* mourning. It's the same with God. Going hard after God takes what we know *about* God and transfers it into the reality of life. We go from understanding His nature to *knowing* Him.

We can see in the Old Testament the "compassionate and gracious God, slow to anger, abounding in love and faithfulness" (Exodus 34:6; Numbers 14:18; Deuteronomy 4:31; Nehemiah 9:17; Psalm 86:5, 15; 108:4; 145:8; Joel 2:13). In the New Testament, evidence of this is seen throughout the Gospels in the character of the Messiah Jesus, God in the flesh, as He moved among the people with care. Jews, Gentiles, and people from all walks of life and religious backgrounds— rich, poor, and the politically astute—each received the same compassion, the same mercy, and the same offer of eternal life.

Throughout the Old Testament, a God of judgment and love is revealed through His creation, standing by His Word, and freeing His people from the bondage of sin. In the New Testament, we see a God of judgment and love in the form of Jesus, unwavering in His convictions, standing by His Word, and freeing people from the bondage of sin.

There are no inconsistencies in the Bible, no contradictions, and despite modern argument and theory, there are no fantasy gods in it. God is real. And He is the same today as He was yesterday, and He will remain unchanged forever. Revealed in sixty-six individual books written on two or three continents, in three different languages, over a period of fifteen hundred years by more than forty authors, and still it remains the most powerful and transformative book ever written. Consistent and unified from beginning to end without contradiction, not constrained or compromised by translations, versions, or semantics, scholars have failed to disprove it time and time again.

I love it. There is no replacement for the peace it brings when I'm anxious or the joy it brings when I am despondent.

A few years ago, I took Beth Moore's example and got in the habit of reading through several different Bible translations at once. Every one of them is marked up with passage notes, circles, pen marks in places that had special meaning for me, and even questions. I even write my own psalms in the margins.

It's my way of talking to God sometimes. Somehow, a new Bible can give me the fresh perspective. And, I enjoy the surprise of new lessons from the same old verses. Somehow there is a mystery in all of this that is sweet and satisfying, challenging the mind and heart to a lot more than simply knowing *about* God. And how exciting! How incredible and how divinely exceptional it is when we see ourselves in the light of His eyes and we begin to change—our perspective, our goals, and our worship. Like clay, the Holy Spirit of God, through His written Word and revelations, changes the Leslie of my life into the Leslie of His vision. And He will do the same for you! Praise God! He is no respecter of persons.

And that's it, really. That's the bottom line for all of us who seek higher living—sound doctrine and the wisdom to apply it.

The Bible is the road that will take you there. So rich and so vital are its stories, that if it is to have any impact on our lives at all, we'll not spend any time at all *just reading it*. We'll spend the rest of our lives deeply entrenched and submerged in it.

Reflection—Enter His Presence Through His Word

The Holy Bible is all God, and no other book reveals Him so vividly. It is God-breathed, so life inheres in it. The purpose of reading the Bible is not only to know the laws of God but to know God; taking aim at the characteristics of God, modeling ourselves to live in the image of Him, and transforming us through the power of influence—seeing Him and wanting to be like the personal God, not a list of facts, virtues, or moral maxims. What characteristics of our holy God do you most embody? Which ones are you aiming at?

An Offered Prayer

Holy Father,

I come today in complete humility and surrender. I am opening your Bible expecting to know you on a deeper level. I want to see your character, your mind, and your ways, so that I can apply them to my life and my living. In thanksgiving, I promise to respond to this knowing in obedience and love to whatever you command of me. I give myself to you now and always. Amen.

6

What Do You Want From My Life, Lord?

God's Divine Design

"Blessed be the Lord my strength which teacheth my hands to war, and my fingers to fight."

—Psalm 144:1

It's the perfect plan. We read the Word of God, know God, know ourselves, are transformed, and then go out and change the world—pretty straightforward, right?

It's flawless, and it all serves God's greater purpose, which is to bring us back into a right relationship with Him and take back every good thing that the enemy of our souls has stolen from us.

I'll explain. In the beginning, we were made in the image of God, to be a perfect reflection of His holiness. As God's representatives, He intended for us to be a dominion people and have the highest authority over the earth, to rule it, control it, and to keep things orderly. Our last command revealed in Genesis was to be fruitful and multiply and replenish the earth (Genesis 1:28).

When Adam sinned, he broke that partnership with God, marred the image of God within, and then passed that broken image on to all of us (Romans 5:12). But God was merciful and prepared. His plan was and is to redeem us, to create for us a new self-image (Ephesians 4:24) and allow us to take back our inheritance and partnership with God.

And so now, rather than living in a perfect garden in perfect communion with a perfect God and having authority over a perfect and yielding earth, our lives have become a war for eternity, and the ultimate "take back" of the earth.

But what about our lives as individuals? What is God's intent?

I'm always surprised when I hear Christians say that life is a test, or a journey to better ourselves, or that it prepares us to meet God in heaven. That view is not biblical at all. It negates what Christ did at Calvary. It implies that through our lives here, we are working for perfection that will make us worthy of heaven, or that we are practicing saying no to sin, which won't even exist in heaven. It makes no sense. The enemy will be cast into the lake of fire, so there will be no more evil or temptation.

When this life is over, we who are in the family of God will live in paradise, as it was originally intended. God's plan of redemption was not just for man, but for the earth as well. He desires to take back His relationship with us and take back the earth for us; evil will be abolished from the earth. And every one of us has a role in that plan.

Now, stay with me.

When God created us and breathed life into us individually, He had a vision for each of us and goals for us to reach—*individually*. To support those goals, He gave us a role in the "take back." Our role is who we are—a functionally unified combination of unique expressions of tone, feelings, perceptions, mental patterns, desires, weaknesses, and traits so highly individualized that it can be likened only to the same uniqueness we see in a physical fingerprint. We are uniquely designed.

Ephesians 2:10 says, "For we are God's handiwork, created in Christ Jesus to do good works, which God prepared in advance for us to do."

Still with me?

I'm a fighter. Always have been. I'm the one you call when you get cheated by a used-car dealership and want your money back. I'm the one you want fighting with you when all weapons are drawn against you and somebody needs to rush the enemy's front line. I'm not the least bit intimidated or put off by confrontation, and when the chips are down, it's all right by me.

When I became a Christian, I prayed and prayed that God would tell me what He wanted me to do with my life and let me know what gifts He had given me. From my very shallow perspective, I decided I needed to change a few things in me. I wanted to be softer spoken and more feminine like my sister Nene. I thought God would surely be more pleased with me and my service to Him if instead of always trying to straighten the ocean, I, for the first time in my life, would learn to just go with the flow.

Yeah, no . . . it didn't work. I am today who I've always been, and there's no changing that. However, what *has* changed are the things I fight for and against, as well as how I use my spiritual weapons.

When I was young, I always had my fists balled up, ready for a fight. My biggest pet peeves were bullies and racial injustices. There were also the daily things that got under my skin and kept the gloves on, but for the most part, I was always ready for a good fight. I was very practical, focused, and diligent in my desire to win.

Today, I am still very practical, focused, and diligent in my desire to win. I still fight injustices, still fight against bullies, and still fight against our enemy who seeks to kill, steal, and destroy. But the battle is no more against flesh and blood; my words are my weapons and tools of destruction, and my time is spent in battle.

God doesn't change our makeup or who we are from the soul, because that part of us is suited specifically for our role in life. He simply grows us up to fit it.

My cousin is a great example. He proudly tells everyone he is a warrior, gifted in the art of war. For the majority of his life, he sold drugs and was also addicted to the drugs he sold. He was in and out of jail constantly, in and out of gangs usually, and committed the types of crimes and acts of violence that most of us only see on television. He was confrontational, arrogant, and violent—the kind of person who, if you saw him coming on one side of the street, you'd cross over to the other side to avoid him.

A little over five years ago, God moved in his heart. My cousin gave himself wholly to God's service. Today, that cousin is one of the most fervent witnesses for God's kingdom I know, walking the streets and being a witness to the homeless and addicted men on skid row in California. He lives there himself. By choice.

My cousin knows this life is war. He battles for the souls of men who are entrapped by strongholds they don't even know exist. And who he is has not changed, but how he applies himself has. He is still gifted in the art of a good fight, still confrontational, and still fearless when it comes to getting it done.

The amazing thing is he never actively sought out what God wanted him to do. Once he gave lordship of his life over to Christ, he just found himself doing it. And it was the same for me. Getting to know Leslie is the second best and most surprising part of my life relationship journey with Jesus Christ.

I searched for years trying to understand *me*. And if I'm being honest, some of the biggest mistakes in my life were made when I was trying to find myself. What I have found, however, is that the best way to find one's *self* is to find God. The best way to understand one's purpose in life is to know God's purpose *for* life. Starting from God, you work your way outward.

You see, God has already purposed for each of us how we fit into His divine design. There is no need to go searching for it; by our very nature and who we are, it *will* seek us out. And that's the simple truth. That to me is one of the best things about finding our place in this war. God has a desired plan for each of our lives, and if you are open to it, He won't let you miss it.

People ask me all the time how to find their calling in life and how I found mine. Perhaps we think God will allow us a preview for acceptance testing and a sign-off. Yeah . . . but no. He won't. God doesn't need our approval of His plans. He only asks our permission to be used. He requires our *yes*.

I don't imagine the same God who is intense enough to send His only Son to die to set us free will keep us in bondage to a search. I don't think He is so much concerned about the areas of service we enter, as long as we serve. Go where your gifts are.

Sometimes it can be easy to forget our divine origins and limit ourselves to our earthly inheritance: family traditions, strongholds, inherent weaknesses. But we are much bigger and more purposeful than that.

We are spirit: unique, powerful, and distinctive through Christ. We each are given a rich legacy of spiritual gifts needed to achieve our individual life mission. At our core, we are already who we need to be, and God is growing us up in our own skin—daily making us more and more in tune to our gifts and character traits in order that we might carry out His appointed plan. There is no need to spend our lives trying to be "stretched" or trying to conform to some image of who we think we *should* be in Christ.

And that's the good news. Because I'm old now, and much too tired, and being stretched by any sense of the imagination is completely out of the question for me. You get what you see—stiff and satisfied to be the person I am.

I discovered completely by accident who Leslie is when someone threw an airplane at the building I was working in. What God had purposed for my life forged ahead. So like my cousin, I simply followed my leader and said yes to opportunities that He gave me to serve Him. That's what has brought me to where I am now.

And it really is as simple as that. Follow your leader into the fight. And fight in your own way, with your own skills, and as best you know how. Some days that fight will be a good fight and other days it may break you down. But keep listening and responding to the prodding, urging, nudging, and whispers that emerge from the Voice in the bush that burns, and keep following.

Your purpose is what your purpose always will be—to live out the directives of God's voice, to respond immediately to the prodding of His Holy Spirit, and to act according to the example of Jesus Christ that sends us to the front lines of a war to take back the earth and free a people enslaved.

Reflection—God's Plan for Your Life

Because of how we were created, our gifts will naturally follow our purpose. Be honest with yourself and think about this: What things are you naturally good at and how do they align with serving God?

An Offered Prayer

Holy Father,

Will you encourage my heart in the things you have given me passion for? And in doing so, help me to be a discipling instrument to walk beside other believers—teaching them to study your Word and modeling the living of it. Only by your divine enablement can I do this.

It is for the glory of God that I desire these things and in the name of my Lord Jesus that I boldly ask. Amen.

Understanding Me

On our farm in Pennsylvania, there were cherry trees which were attacked by little parasites of some sort. A parasite would get into a little branch, pierce the bark and exude a gum. Then the branch would get a knot on it and bend. All over the trees were those little bent places with gummy knots. After two or three years, those cherry trees would not bloom. If they did, the blooms usually dropped early and the cherries did not come to fruition. If the blooms did not drop early, the cherries would be flat and undeveloped or only red on one side.

My father was not too interested in fruit. He was interested in cattle, horses, and grain. If my father had known how he could have protected those trees before they got into that wretched condition and properly sprayed or treated them, he could have gotten rid of the worms and bugs and saved the trees and fruit.

I believe that a pastor who is content with a vineyard that is not at its best is not a good husbandman. It is my prayer

67

that we may be a healthy and fruitful vineyard and that we may be an honor to the Well Beloved, Jesus Christ the Lord, and that He might go before the Father and say, "These are mine for whom I pray, and they have heard the Word and have believed on Me."

I pray that we might fit into the high priestly prayer of John 17, and that we would be a church after Christ's own heart so that in us He might see the travail of His soul and be satisfied. In order for us to be a vine like that, there must be basic purity. Each one must have a great purity of heart. I believe there are no emotional experiences that do not rest upon great purity of heart. No one can impress me or interest me in any kind of spiritual manipulation if his or her heart is not pure—even if it is raising the dead. Sound righteousness in conduct must be at the root of all valid spiritual experience.[1]

—A. W. Tozer

Father,

Thank you for the opportunity to bear good fruit— that we can go into the fields and gather more for you. I pray now in Jesus' name that you will fill us up with your words, your wisdom, and your anointing. Cause us, Lord, by your Holy Spirit, to understand who we are in your kingdom, that we might reflect that image to a dying world, which bears no fruit.

Fill us up, Father, and send us out. And be glorified in all that we do.

In Jesus' name. Amen.

7

Why Do Crazy Things Keep Happening to Me?

Spiritually Punk'd

"Fight the good fight of the faith. Take hold of the eternal life to which you were called when you made your good confession in the presence of many witnesses."

—1 Timothy 6:12

We win! Guaranteed!

Yes, through the blood of Jesus Christ, the victory in this war has already been declared. Satan is fighting from a position of defeat. He cannot win no matter how hard he tries. So he has but one objective: to thwart the power of God in our lives and subsequently keep us from being on the offensive against the darkness.

His strategy is to deceive us into believing that the fight with him is about something more than what it is. He lies. He distracts. He deceives. He prowls around like a roaring lion looking for someone to devour (1 Peter 5:8). And all the time with no real power over us!

So why does it feel like we are always in a fight? And how do we know if we are under spiritual attack?

Well, it begins like this: You meet the Lord Jesus Christ, you receive Him as your Savior and Lord, He loads you up with weapons of warfare, and the fight begins. From that moment on, you are under attack and the battle rages day in and day out. It never stops. Dreams change, people change, and the road is laden with twists and turns that take you to unexpected events and enemies you have to focus in on to see.

When we say yes to the Lord, we say yes to a life lived out on a battlefield. We have to fight for our peace, our security, our freedom, our joy, and sometimes even eternity. Though most of us attribute all life conflicts to the work of the devil, from the moment we become true followers of Jesus Christ and God is visible in us, we face the attacks of a powerful partnership between the world system, demonic forces, and our own flesh—all conspiring to make our lives fruitless.

You see, being a Christian is a lot more than a religious title. It means we are joint heirs with Jesus Christ and the Holy Spirit of God lives within us. We live as Jesus did with a goal to loose the chains of injustice and untie the cords of the yoke, to set the oppressed free and break every yoke (Isaiah 58). There is no middle ground.

We say yes to godliness and no to superficiality and religious practices steeped in traditions, because I've never seen tradition set a man free or religion give him life.

In fact, God exists where religion will not tread. This is the Christian life—walking always in the spirit of truth and opened up to a whole new realm of supernatural living, surprising twists, unexpected life lessons, and paradigm-shattering events that change the world around us. Bless the Lord! This is living!

Oftentimes we encourage one another to "hang in there"—asserting that things are going to get better. And so we are often surprised when it just gets worse.

Over the years, I have talked with people who have been disheartened because they believed that salvation would be a magic carpet ride to eternal bliss. They, and no doubt many before them, expected God to slay life's dragons for them and keep them from all discord and discomfort.

But again, serving God is not for the faint of heart. The peace that God offers is not without conflict. So if you came to God expecting a walk in the park, you came with your eyes wide shut. You *should* expect turmoil. Expect disruption. Expect people to hate you. Expect lies to be told. Expect the unexpected and think it not strange when it comes:

> Dear friends, do not be surprised at the fiery ordeal that has come on you to test you, as though something strange were happening to you.
>
> —1 Peter 4:12

God promises to give us peace through our difficulties, not instead of them. Again, our Christian life is a life of war. So peace does not mean the absence of conflict. Peace is the ability to rest in God straight through it.

One of the most effective weapons the enemy uses against our minds is the suggestion that we as Christians should have carefree lives and anything other than that is not God's will. We then shift our focus from fighting the good fight, as the Word tells us to do (1 Timothy 6:12), to avoiding one.

We bite down hard on Satan's lies and they keep us in bondage to fears and insecurities that feed addictions, depression that triggers mental illness, and broken relationships that threaten to affect our families for generations.

> The god of this age has blinded the minds of unbelievers, so that they cannot see the light of the gospel that displays the glory of Christ, who is the image of God.
>
> —2 Corinthians 4:4

> For though we walk in the flesh, we do not war after the flesh: For the weapons of our warfare are not carnal, but mighty through God to the pulling down of strong holds; casting down imaginations, and every high thing that exalteth itself against the knowledge of God, and bringing into captivity every thought to the obedience of Christ.
>
> —2 Corinthians 10:3–5 KJV

And now the fight gets good. The enemy takes it up a notch and wars against us on every level. He uses distraction, deceit, and probably his most effective weapon yet: our ignorance of (or refusal to concede to) the fact that he even exists. Certainly, the most formidable enemy is one we cannot see.

A few years ago, a video game called Mortal Kombat was all the rage. I loved playing it. The street-fighting game turned movie pitted three good guys against a legion of bad guys in an intergalactic martial-arts tournament to determine the fate of the human race.

The special effects are amazing, taking the good guys to a remote island where, following the failure of several previous human defenders, mankind's last chance rests in the hands of a vengeance-minded hero, Liu Kang. (Cue: music.)

When the final battle begins, fists fly and jumping kicks are everywhere. All during the fight, Liu Kang's enemy is toying with Kang's mind to weaken him—showing him his fears and whispering his weakness. Bloodied and struggling to breathe, Liu Kang is one kick away from defeat when he begins to believe he is destined to win. Then suddenly the enemy's voice is silenced by the truth, and everything else around the two fighters fades to black. Liu stands to his feet. He wipes the blood from his mouth, broadens his stance, and delivers the final and fatal blow. Yay! And it's just like that in life.

In real life, once we accept the truth of who God created us to be, and the authority that we have through Christ's shed blood, the victory in battle is ours.

But when we give ear to the lies of the enemy, we start believing things like: "A drink will work faster than prayer"; "One pull of that joint won't hurt"; "Your wife is cheating on you"; "Your son is just like his father—no good"; "Go ahead, kiss that woman, you don't have to go any further." He tricks us into believing that the very things that will kill us spiritually are harmless and that he himself has the power to cause us to move in that direction. But he doesn't. The enemy has no power or authority over our behavior without our permission. We just have to say *no*.

I used to be very active in street ministry. There were times I'd approach someone's home to talk about God's offer of salvation and be met with hostility. Other times I was welcomed.

On one occasion, I went to the home of a practicing witch. She was known in the neighborhood for feeding different concoctions to people and casting spells. As I talked with her, I started to feel a little itchy, like creepy crawlies were all over my skin and in my hair. I felt a sharp pain in my chest. It seemed to move through my chest and puncture my heart. I couldn't breathe, let alone speak. For a second or two or even three, I was terrified. I clutched my chest. My mind raced through every demon-binding Scripture that I could think of. But what came to mind so clearly was to pray in tongues. And so I did—aloud.

The pain left me instantly.

There have also been times when I was speaking about spiritual warfare in churches and the microphone died. I've given interviews about God's power in my life and the cameras wouldn't function properly or lights flickered, until I asked the Lord to remove the obstacles.

On more than one occasion, I have experienced manifestations of demonic opposition and the overcoming power of God's Holy Spirit. And I believe without doubt that we have to *know* that no power in heaven or on earth can prevent the power of God (Psalm 135:6). God has equipped us and dressed us for battle. Paul testifies in 2 Corinthians, "Though we live in the world, we do not wage war as the world does" (10:3). Later he tells us, "Our struggle is not against flesh and blood, but against the rulers, against the authorities, against the powers of this dark world and against the spiritual forces of evil in heavenly realms," and to "be strong in the Lord and in his mighty power. Put on the full armor of God, so that you can take your stand against the devil's schemes" (Ephesians 6:10–12). And while we are told several times to put on our armor or take up our weapons, there is no place in the sixty-six books of the Bible that tells us to take off the armor or put down our weapons. We are always suited up, always with our weapons, and always engaged in battle.

And while for some people the opposition is subtle and seemingly uneventful, others might actually feel malevolence, and still others have been oppressed for so long that they no longer are aware of the attacks.

When my mother died, and I went away to college, I felt an onslaught of wickedness that I had not felt in my entire life. I was confused, depressed, and even violent at times. I experimented with drinking and even drugs. At first I passed it off as grief. But when I started reading my mother's favorite Scriptures and listening to tapes of her singing, the feelings of rage left me. The confusion and depression soon lifted, as well. But it wasn't until the attack stopped that I realized what was going on and the intensity of it.

Writing this book has been another lesson in warfare. I lost the first six chapters within the first few weeks of writing, and when I attempted to rewrite them, I fought one distraction after another. My thoughts were jumbled, I had bad dreams, and when I tried to read my Bible, I was suddenly sleepy. It didn't make sense.

My concern led me to ask my brother, Pastor Lawrence Haskin, if he thought I was under attack. His response: "What difference does it make? Just stay faithful."

And that's the simple truth of it. That's the answer in a nutshell: no long explanations or drawn out conclusions. It doesn't matter which enemy we are facing, whether we are fighting the enemy of flesh, the enemy of world forces, or demonic ones, our charge is to stay faithful and in the fight.

What does it matter what the enemy is or isn't doing? The truth is that the war continues to rage around us. We simply have to remain faithful to God. We have to continue to fast and pray. Continue to worship and live upright lives before the Lord.

I know from whence I speak. There are times when my life is so crazy and filled with such random spiritual events that I actually stop, look up toward heaven, and ask if I'm being "punk'd" by God. At other times, my life is so peaceful and so good that I sleep like a baby.

In hindsight, I realize I've got a couple of new dents in my "fender" and I've been bruised a bit. But it is what it is. My charge in my Christian walk with God is just that.

I open my eyes every morning with my focus on God but my enemy in my sights. True living in the Spirit is a lifestyle of readiness. Everything you do is warfare. You are either preparing to fight, training to fight, actually fighting, or analyzing the last fight in order to win the next. And if I'm being honest, I have to say that the best days of my life have been these latter days spent on the battlefield with my Lord, fighting the good fight of faith that is all together unpredictable, inspiring, enlightening, crazy, scary, amazing, and absolutely wonderful. That's a lot of adjectives, I know, but "it's all good."

Because I know that at the end of the day, when this war is over, I will bow my knees before an Almighty God who will look at me with a smile in His eyes and raise His mighty hand to me and say, "Well done, my good and faithful servant. Well done."

Reflection—Pick Your Battles

Sometimes our fiercest battles are with our flesh first, followed by battles against the world's influence, and finally with the devil's minions. It seems interesting that the source we attribute most to our battles—the devil—is the least contributive. We give him more credit than he deserves. Think about your most frequent battles; what are you *really* fighting?

Also, read Isaiah 58 and reflect on how it ties in to spiritual warfare.

An Offered Prayer

Dear Lord,

I ask only that you will open my eyes to the tactics of my enemy so that I can defeat it in whatever form it takes . . . even if it is my own self. Amen.

8

Why Do Christians Still Struggle With Addictions?

Get Off the Sidelines

"It is for freedom that Christ has set us free. Stand firm, then, and do not let yourselves be burdened again by a yoke of slavery."

—Galatians 5:1

To hear God's voice say "Well done" should be the ultimate motivation for every born-again Christian. It means you have fought the good fight and won.

Because, let's face it, living a defeated Christian life is the worst place on the planet to be. It is dark, dreadful, and consistent only in the way that it never gets better. You are miserable all the time and life never gives up her joy for you.

It's like being on the sidelines of the best game in town and watching everyone else win while you are stuck in the muck.

And so it must come as quite a shock to a great many of us who don't have the miracle deliverances, when we realize that becoming a born-again believer doesn't mean God will always show up in our lives, cast out every bad behavior and spirit that is unlike Him, and immediately change us into integral, contented believers who live His abundant life of promise. Butterflies won't suddenly land on our hands and flowers won't bloom in dark places. In fact, at first, nothing changes. Our lifestyle is still the same, our habits are still the same, and our circumstances are the same.

If, before we came to Christ, we lied, we'll continue to lie. We'll still use drugs, drink, swear, smoke, and indulge in many other bad habits inappropriate for a Christian life.

Even God's supernatural deliverance will only change us from the inside. The rest is up to us.

My father always said we are the sum total of our behaviors. In other words, we are what we do. If we lie, we are a liar. If we steal, we are a thief. If we have friends who smoke and drink and cause trouble, our life will always be filled with drama. If we are repeatedly promiscuous, life will always be filled with emotional heartbreak and the possibility of disease and pregnancy. If we spend money on drinking and using drugs, life will be financially insufficient, unsatisfying, not to mention dysfunctional.

But joy, joy, this is *not* the life God wants for us. Jeremiah 29:11 says, "'For I know the plans I have for you,' declares the Lord, 'plans to prosper you and not to harm you, plans to give you hope and a future.'" In John 10:10, Jesus tells us He has come that we might have abundant life. The promise here is that we can live superior, superabundant spiritual lives that are empowered by the indwelling of His Holy Spirit.

When we receive the gift of God's Holy Spirit, things begin to move. He creates in us the desire to live better lives and to be transformed by the renewing of our minds (Romans 12:2). He meticulously points out to us behaviors that bind us to unproductive and dysfunctional living. But He doesn't *make* us change; the work of eliminating those behaviors belongs to us. In order to change our lives, we have to first change ourselves. The Holy Spirit of God empowers us to do that. And if we want to live prosperous and healthy lives, we have to put away behaviors that work against that goal.

You see, most of life is habitual. We do the same things today that we did yesterday, the day before, and probably every day for the last month. We have our morning rituals, our patterns of speech, even our preferred spot on the bed. Some things we do so often and so routinely that they become automatic. It's like driving the same route every day to and from work for so long that we do it mindlessly, or like a river that flows through a canyon. The longer a habit continues, the more deeply it becomes ingrained in us, making it harder to change. The longer bad behavior persists, the more likely we are to accept it and ignore the accompanying problems. I see this happening all the time.

A few months ago, I was speaking at a weekend seminar. My topic was "Life Without Limits." After a session about the importance of letting go, a woman told me that even after repeatedly asking God for deliverance from a few lingering addictions, she was still struggling. She was concerned that I didn't really understand the power of addictions—that they are a disease that requires treatment, and my seminar should approach the subject with a gentler hand.

"Stop drinking the Kool-Aid," I told her. "Nobody can be addicted to a bad habit." I went on to say that for her to argue that she can be addicted to what really is a bad habit implies that some external, destructive stimulus has pathological power over her and that it dictates what she does.

The truth is, when we say that we are addicted to a bad habit, we imply that we are not in control of our own lives; sin is. We give ourselves an alibi to rationalize our subliminal and compulsively devoted pursuit of selfish satisfactions or to cover up some pain or dissociative lie. (Try saying that fast!)

You see, the Bible instructs us to live sober-minded lives and to be in control of our bodies (1 Corinthians 15:34). It wouldn't give us that instruction if it were possible that some external thing could control us. Unless you have robot arms, robot legs, and a robot brain—all controlled by a grand master—habits and addictions need your express permission to be performed because they are performed by you.

The better argument is that our old sin nature, the nature that was in control before Christ came into our lives, is a greater motivator than the discipline a life in Christ demands. When scientists or medical doctors tell us that drugs or alcohol cause chemical reactions in the brain that lead to addictions, we have to reject that explanation and know that when the Holy Spirit of God comes to live in us, we become new creatures and He sets us free from our old nature. "If anyone is in Christ, he is a new creation; the old has gone, the new has come!" (2 Corinthians 5:17 NIV1984).

The bottom line is that an addiction supports a habit that feeds pain and lies. And appetite grows on what it is fed. The more we indulge the lie, the more it demands. The more it demands, the more the soul becomes "tolerant" of the stimulus that feeds it and we continue the bad behavior—by our own choice. And since there is no limit to the depth of emotional pain a person can endure, or a direct route to exposure of the lies embedded in one's soul, there is no limit to the extent of satisfying our bad habits (again, our choice).

What is the key to freedom then? Change your mind, change your thinking, and your habits will conform. Stop your bad habits and you stop the addictions as well. Despite modern theology and so-called tolerance therapy (which support addictions, bad habits, and excuses not to bring our bodies and minds into submission to the will of God), God has given us authority over the enemy and the chains that he uses to hold us captive. *Walk away.*

Time and again the enemy steals *our* anointed, binds them to destructive behaviors, and keeps them distanced from their right to live God's promises.

I know I'm going to be challenged on this, but deliverance, my friends, is not a journey. It's a state of freedom that God grants. It is not something that we work to achieve. God delivers us when He frees us. And when the Son sets you free, you are free indeed (John 8:36). All we have to do is decide to change and find a motivator that is greater than the old nature.

When I was about sixteen, I was introduced to shoplifting. The first time I stole something, I was shaking in my boots when I left the store. But the more I did it, the more I enjoyed that feeling of excitement and the easier it was to do. I shoplifted until it became a habit.

One day I decided to skip classes and go shopping. Money was not a consideration for me as I was prepared with an oversized sweater and a large backpack in tow, into which several items found their way before the afternoon was even half over.

Leaving the store was a piece of cake, until I wandered past the shoe section and met my first love: a pair of Donna Karan stoned wedges. They were beautiful. With a masterfully woven heel and a black lace strap that wrapped around the ankle, they screamed, "Take me home!" I had to have them. I tried them on, left them on, and headed toward the door. Those shoes made me feel like I was walking on a cloud. Even taller.

Though my heart pounded from the adrenaline rush, I kept moving. I could see freedom just a few feet away. I took a deep breath, got ready to step over that buzzer thingy with my fabulous new shoes, and out of nowhere stepped the biggest, scariest-looking guy I had ever laid eyes on. He looked as if he'd stepped right out of a highway patrol movie, Smokey himself.

From my four-foot-eleven-inch stature, he seemed to be a gigantic seven-and-a-half-foot-tall man with massive shoulders and huge hands that wrapped around my entire arm like it was a stick. He was wearing sunglasses—inside—and sported a big black leather jacket, finger-release leather gloves, wrist bands, a black flipper cap, and black leather knee-high boots. He wore a military-like belt loaded with weapons. He had handcuffs, a flashlight, a whipping stick, Taser gun, pepper spray, hairspray, truth syrup, and maple syrup. I think I even saw a whip and chains and keys to the Batmobile. I almost fainted when he spoke.

He took me to jail. I did not pass go and definitely did not collect two hundred dollars.

My one phone call was to my mom. The officer talked to her for me, and all I remember after he hung up was he and his partners laughing but saying they felt sorry for me. I knew I was in trouble. I sat for hours crying and dreading my mother's arrival. I hoped that as the time passed, Mom's heart would miraculously soften and she wouldn't kill her baby girl, or that my dad would leave work and come instead, which wasn't likely, but in the spirit of "keeping hope alive" . . .

When Mom finally arrived, it was on the winds of a firestorm. That woman grabbed me by my collar, and the breaking of bad habits began. (This was back in the day when it was okay to spank your children.)

To this day I don't know how my legs made it from the jail to the car. But I do recall that my mother spanked me all the way home . . . from the car, to the house, up the front stairs, through the living room, past my brothers and sisters, out the back door into the yard and straight on to Neverland.

I think I was twenty-one when that spanking finally ended. I'm kidding, but needless to say, I learned a quick and valuable lesson that day about bad habits and the motivation for breaking them.

Mine was the sting of a tightly wound belt and a few stern words of encouragement from my mom that have stayed with me until this day. As it is written, "Withhold not correction from the child: for if thou beatest him with the rod, he shall not die. Thou shalt beat him with the rod, and shalt deliver his soul from hell" (Proverbs 23:13–14 KJV).

Sometimes pain can be a great motivator.

Now that I think of it, perhaps my mom was onto something. Perhaps sometimes we learn best from those things that hurt us the most. Whether it comes via the ache of sitting in the dark because you spent the money on drugs or alcohol or too much shopping, or from the rejection you feel because your friends no longer take your calls because your conversations are filled with gossip. Whatever moves you to the decision to change, God has provided a means of escape. But the decision to walk through the door is yours.

Know that your inheritance is not a life lived in bondage. Now go, get off the sidelines and be free in Jesus' name.

Reflection—Delayed Gratification

Napoleon Hill, who wrote widely on personal development, wrote, "Self-discipline begins with the mastery of your thoughts. If you don't control what you think, you can't control what you do. Simply, self-discipline enables you to think first and act afterward." What is your thought life and in what ways does having intimacy with Christ help toward your goal of discipline and eliminating sinful behavior?

An Offered Prayer

Heavenly Father,

Your Word tells us we should have the mind of Christ. This is discipline, honor, and respect. Help me, dear Lord, to practice discipline in my life and be more honoring to you with my behavior. Forgive me. And give me the courage to admit my responsibility for my own actions and the strength to take control. Amen.

9

How Do I Know
What My Gifts Are?

Shoes, Glorious Shoes!

"Now about the gifts of the Spirit, brothers and sisters,
I do not want you to be uninformed."

—1 Corinthians 12:1

Speaking of freedom, I was in London not long ago when
I heard the news that Stuart Weitzman, shoe genius and
master craftsman extraordinaire, would not be designing his
million-dollar shoes for the stars to wear at the year's Oscars.
It felt like somebody cancelled Christmas for Leslie and the
shoe genie had taken me to jail.

In case you aren't familiar with Mr. Weitzman, he designs
the most amazing shoes, ornamented with millions of dollars

of jewels and fabulous sparkles for celebrities to wear on the red carpet.

Well, during my stay in London, I was blessed to see a pair of his shoes up close. And to say I felt the favor of God on me would be an understatement. You see, I am anointed for shoes. Like many of my gender, I have a deep and meaningful relationship with fashion for the feet. I'm a "shoe-nista." I have mastered the art of the shoe purchase, the shoe selection, the wearing of the shoe, and the shoe categorization.

Here are my rules: Never buy shoes without trying on the left foot. Never pick a shoe that is the current fad-only style. Never wear a thirty-minute shoe to a three-hour event. Never try hovering in a pair of kitten-heel ostrich-feather-trimmed mules. It cannot be done! And always, always, always know your date pump from your church pump because the shoes will make the outfit.

I can be wearing just about any piece of clothing at all, even the dullest piece, but the minute I put on a pair of Azzedine Alaia or Zanotti pumps—Poof!—magic happens. Honestly, there isn't one pair of shoes in my closet that doesn't work that magic. And even though classic Chanel always has its place, anytime, as a rule, the funkier the shoe the better. It doesn't matter if they're covered in sparkles or animal print, bright colors or earth tones, lace up, zip up, or sling-backs. No matter the fabrics, materials, clasps, buckles, straps, or jewels, I am all about the shoes. Oh, yes, there's no stopping the abracadabra. I am excited by everything shoe. My friends buy me prints of shoes. They give me miniature shoes, shoe molds, and even shoe cookies. When I want to reward myself for something, I buy shoes. When I celebrate, I buy shoes. When I'm sad, I cheer myself with . . . guess what? Shoes.

So when Jesus showed up in my dream a few years ago carrying a brand-new pair of stunning shiny gold clogs, it was no surprise. In the dream, He handed the clogs to me. I took them in my hands and just held them, admiring them. I kept telling Him how beautiful they were. I was overwhelmed and humbled somehow, but I just kept standing there, holding the shoes and never putting them on. It didn't make any sense. Normally, I can't wait to wear the new smell out of a shoe. To me, a nice shoe is a piece of art that can only fully be appreciated when seen on a foot. It feels good to hold them and look at them, but the goal is to own them and wear them.

Anyway, back to the dream. Baffled and even a bit disturbed by my behavior in the dream, I asked an expert, my friend Tiffany. It's worth mentioning that while Tiffany is gifted in the area of dream interpretation, she is also a shoenista herself, so I felt confident she was the perfect person to consult.

Tiffany told me that from what she has learned, the color gold in dreams indicates the dreamer is a healer. The shoes implied a journey to an unknown destination in life. God giving them to me represented the impartation of a new spiritual gift from Him. She said my hesitance revealed, on some level, either my readiness or lack thereof. All together, God was giving me a spiritual gift that would take me places that I wasn't expecting to go. The fact that I admired the shoes but wouldn't wear them indicated I was not readily accepting of my new gifts and roles. And even though I thought God's gift was incredibly beautiful, it was more comfortable for me to hold them than to put them on and walk in them—to walk in a new anointing.

Come on, really?

Every true shoe-nista knows you never even attempt to walk in public in a pair of brand-new shoes without categorizing them. And you can't just take a pair of shoes from somebody and put them right on. There are style considerations and life-style considerations and even the statement the shoes make.

As Marilyn Monroe once said, "Give a girl the right shoes, and she can conquer the world."

The more I pushed against Tiffany's interpretation, the more it set in my mind. I started thinking about Moses. I could now easily relate to the way he questioned God's call. I kept thinking, *Hey, this is ME we're talking about.* God had to be mistaking me for somebody else, or even worse, maybe I just wasn't hearing him correctly. After all, God had delivered me from extreme fear and post-traumatic stress disorder years ago, so hearing voices was not entirely beyond my scope of the real. Just kidding. But even if it was true that God wanted me to go forth in service to His people, I had a distorted self-image and no idea of how to employ the gifts He had given me.

Those were pretty big shoes to fill.

About a year later, I was visiting a friend's church, minding my own business and enjoying the flow of the Holy Spirit, when I noticed a man in the congregation who was losing his hair. I assumed it was probably because of chemotherapy. My heart was so heavy for him that I felt compelled to pray. As I did, I was overwhelmed with compassion. My heart pounded, and I wept. I poured myself out before God like never before.

When it was all over, nothing in particular happened right away, except I felt a sense of confidence.

Six months later, I was back at that church for a harvest ceremony and I was approached by that same man. But this time he had a full head of hair and a glowing complexion. He stood strong and straight and confident. I recognized him immediately, and I was so happy to see what God had done.

The man told me God had completely healed him of cancer. It blew my mind. PRAISE GOD!

I was excited, but still I resisted the Lord's promptings just a bit. In my eyes those were pretty big shoes.

Then finally, after a trillion tears, a million "Why me, Lord?" prayers, and questions to almost everyone I knew about healing and gifts in the body of Christ, it finally started to click. I have no right to withhold any act of love from the huge population of people desperate to know love.

Freedom from bondage opens the doors to freedom in service to our Lord. It acts as a catalyst to move us into a place where we want the same freedoms for others that we enjoy. It's a calling, and God prepares us to answer the call. Not only by placing the desires for ministry in our hearts but also by placing the necessary spiritual gifts in our care. The apostle Paul explains in Galatians 5:13 that we are "called to be free. But do not use your freedom to indulge the flesh; rather, serve one another humbly in love."

Our gifts are freely given to us and should be freely dispensed to help strengthen others. Though God chose to use me to serve in His kingdom, it's not about me. It's about the person sitting next to me in the pew who is battling addictions, or the single mom with three children all screaming in the line at the grocery store, or the homeless family on the corner being crushed by depression.

The gifts that He trusts to our care are vividly reflected in the characteristics of His love, and we have no right to withhold His love from His people. The aim of these gifts is that in everything God might be glorified through Jesus Christ, that a broken world might come to know His faithfulness and His love for them, all while being assured that He withholds no good thing from them. We are to be His outstretched arms and His voice of hope. And for me, there is nothing more thrilling, more joyful, more meaningful, more satisfying than to find our niche in the eternal unfolding of God's glory.

I want to live a life being filled by God and poured out over His people.

And that's my message as I travel internationally, praying for the sick and those enslaved. As I continue to write, it's all about living and fighting for the life God intends us to have.

My life lessons have all been learned by doing. But even with constant practice, I'm still far from comfortable in this space. I might look steady, like I have it all together, but this is all done with mirrors. I still find myself sometimes holding on when I should be letting go, and looking for the expected end rather than the appointed one. Over and over again, I promise myself that next time I'll be immediately obedient to the voice of God. Yet in my human form, I sometimes forget that hope is faith's substance. And though I might struggle with heights a bit, in the end, my focus is on staying vertical in these new shoes and walking beyond the constraints of my own mind—breaking free of the fear of stumbling.

Because if you think about it, it's fear that keeps us all walking in the safe old flats instead of strutting in the brand-new, high-heeled, spectacular shoes.

Our stumbling is gonna be worth it one day!

Still, when we find ourselves in the presence of the Lord, when life has been fully lived and nothing has been thrown away, when we meet to tell our stories and compare notes, I will have to admit life is always a little bit better with a pair of good shoes.

Reflection—Recognizing Your Gifts

Our gifts are freely given to us by God and should be freely shared in our service to God for strengthening others. Our gifts follow our calling and purpose. So in identifying your gifts, write down what you are naturally good at. How can you use these gifts to further the kingdom?

An Offered Prayer

Heavenly Father,

I want my life to be pleasing to you. Fill my cup, Lord. Then send me out to your people, so that I can pour myself out for you. And in this, that you will be glorified. Be glorified in all that I do. In Jesus' name. Amen.

10

Why Am I Still Single?

Relationship Status—"It's Complicated"

"But since sexual immorality is occurring, each man should have sexual relations with his own wife, and each woman with her own husband. The husband should fulfill his marital duty to his wife, and likewise the wife to her husband."

—1 Corinthians 7:2–3

All my best friends are married. They tell me all the time they wouldn't be in my single shoes these days for anything in the world. Truth is, being single today is much too hard. There seems to be this unspoken belief or social stigma that implies singleness needs to be healed.

Books like *How to Be in Relationship* and *How to Be Comfortable in Your Single Skin* sell like hot cakes. Singles clubs, singles dances, and even singles churches are popping up everywhere—all designed to fix someone who's not even broken.

But talking about acceptable relationship status is another matter altogether. This most certainly is broken. I remember back in the day when being single was fun. A man would buy flowers and take a girl to dinner and meet her parents and even go to church with the family. And years before that, men sat in the parlor when they called on a young lady. And they were chaperoned.

These days, social networking sites and Internet dating speed things up until it's almost impossible to keep up with the pace of courting, if there still is such a thing. People don't meet organically anymore, they tweet. Nobody checks the box that asks, "Will you be my girlfriend?" It's all just assumed. If you want to talk, you update your status. If you want to meet someone nice, you update your profile on five different social networking sites and hope "the one" gets *twitter*pated and follows you offline. Back in the day, something like that would be felony stalking; now it's just my relationship status. It's complicated.

And saying you're not single these days doesn't necessarily mean you're married. It can mean you're in a relationship. Saying that you're going out with someone doesn't necessarily mean that you're actually going anywhere at all. It also means you're in a relationship. It's confusing. We've turned the single life over to the hands of our younger generation and they've ruined it.

I miss the days when you had one phone number, and one answering machine; and that one answering machine had one cassette tape, and that one cassette tape either had a message from the guy or it didn't. Now you just have to go around checking all these different portals just to get rejected by seven different technologies. It's exhausting.[1]

Being single is harder now than it ever was. Especially for those of us who are devout Christians. Who does a single Christian date in a world where you can't tell who's really single anymore (or really a Christian)? And what does it mean to be Christian and single in this modern age? Do we follow the same rules of the world and hope for the best, or do we insert our credit cards and pay that whopping thirty-nine-dollar monthly membership fee and hope the computer can find us a good match.

Personally, I've tried it. It doesn't work. eHarmony looked all over the world and found not one match suitable for my personality. And frankly, I'm not surprised. I'm a peculiar people (1 Peter 2:9 KJV). And technology, even as advanced as it is, cannot begin to calculate and match the chemical requirements of love.

There's just nothing like that warm fuzzy feeling you get on that first chance encounter with "the one" and then wondering if he likes you back. Or the stumble and three-second regroup of your composure after you notice that he noticed you from across the room. Woo-hoo! Joy. Joy.

I want those awkward moments. I want the guy who shows up at my door with a dozen red roses and at the end of the date stares deeply into my eyes. I want the one who is not afraid to sing to me in a restaurant, laugh out loud, or raise his hands in praise to God. Just *once* I want my courtship to be like one of those old black-and-white movies, preferably one with a really awesome musical number for no apparent reason, and the next thing I know, I'm ducking rice while leaving a huge church in a really big and beautiful wedding gown. The End.

Perhaps I'm just a bit of a romantic . . . the last of a dying breed. Still, I wonder what ever happened to romance.

I watch the new breed of singles today busying their lives and moving relationships along so fast that they have no idea what they're getting into. Even in the best cases, they are spending less time serving in ministry and less time getting to know God and more time hanging around with friends, patiently waiting for God to cause them to stumble into the person of their dreams. And it works out well for some, all except the patiently waiting part.

It's not a well-kept secret that a lot of single Christians today are "getting ahead" of the dating curve and do not abstain from sexual contact. And they show no shame. I've heard people justify their sin by twisting the meaning of 1 Corinthians 7:9 ("If they cannot control themselves, they should marry, for it is better to marry than to burn with passion") to claim that God created some people who cannot control themselves sexually. And it is increasingly more common for Christians to believe, and even teach others, that if intercourse is not achieved, it's not sex.

But we can't have it both ways. Either it's sex and we can't control ourselves, or it's not sex and we can. And the use of 1 Corinthians as a defense is just plain wrong, otherwise that verse would contradict other verses that tell us to exercise self-control. And God does not instigate confusion, nor does He introduce contradiction into His body.

Sure, it would be a lot easier if the Bible spelled it all out for us and said something like, "Thou shalt have but one boyfriend, and it is he who shall take thee out on three dates, and then after a fortnight, he must propose marriage . . . and with thy lips together thou mayest kiss, but with thy lips parted thou shalt not kiss. Moreover, above the shoulders thou shalt touch freely, but below the shoulders thou shalt not touch."

But it doesn't work like that. There are no laws in the Bible about dating. But there *are* some pretty good biblical principles that we should live by. For example, we are told to be holy (1 Peter 1:16), to keep our bodies as temples and not pollute them with sin, to have control over ourselves and to flee from sexual immorality (1 Corinthians 6:18–19). The stories in the Bible bear witness to those principles as we glimpse relationships that honored God and led to marriage, like Jacob's, and Moses', and even Joseph and Mary. None of these men was with their wives sexually until after they were married.

God expects us to honor Him in our behavior as well as in our bodies. Again, there are no exceptions. This is the rule.

Now, I'm not claiming to be an angel, just honest. I've not been given any gold standard awards of excellence in Christian conduct myself. But my life is lived out loud and above board. Sure, I've made the decision to spend long hours on the phone at night and risk inappropriate conversation rather than hang the phone up and face the screams of loneliness. I've had the visits to my home that could have gotten a bit too cozy when I should have gone for that long walk in the park. And there was a Mr. Wonderful once who tried to convince me that since we were dating, we were not single anymore, and because we were not single, we could do some things that were "technically" not forbidden.

Now that sounds a little too much like the same conversation that old serpent had in the garden with Eve, right? "Surely, God didn't say you couldn't take that fruit . . . "

Get behind me, Satan!

I want my magic night and I want my integrity intact when I get there. When I walk down that aisle toward the man I love, I want him to see his own reflection in my eyes. I want him to know that his secrets—the touch of my hand, the softness of my lips, and every private and intimate thing a woman shares with her husband—have all been safe with me. No other man knows.

'Cause let's be real, ladies, once we have sex, it's impossible to go back. We can't un-open that door or cross back over that line. We'll never be the same. We damage our souls and put ourselves at the mercy of sin's consequences—lying to cover it up, hoping we didn't get a disease or worse, feeling used and ugly, praying nobody finds out, feeling shame before God, becoming more bitter and then more impatient in the wait.

I don't want to lecture you. That is not why I write. The truth is that your body belongs to you; you can do with it whatever you choose. But is it worth the price of your emotional health?

That's what makes it a sin, you know—the damage it does to the soul. Premarital sex is not wrong because God is withholding something good from us. It's wrong because God is protecting us from something bad. You see, by design, sex joins two hearts as one. There are no exceptions.

Song of Songs 4:9 describes the vulnerability of expressing romantic desire to another when it says, "You have stolen my heart, my sister, my bride; you have stolen my heart with one glance of your eyes."

When romantic desire and attraction are expressed and reciprocated, it "steals the heart" and makes it vulnerable.

Without the commitment and resultant security of marriage, our hearts will be crushed every time.

And just like that, the dream for a "happily ever after" begins its slow walk down the long green mile. And the longer the walk, the further down that road you go, the easier it gets to just stop dreaming and stop hoping and stop waiting.

Now, this is usually the part in the movie when I'm crying for the woman who wants so desperately to be in love, and the man of her dreams, whom she doesn't see, is buying his ticket to get to her. I'm sitting up in my seat by now, cheering him on and screaming at the screen, telling her, "Wait, he's coming!"

Surely we all feel that rush that comes from wanting the happy-ending story. But it makes for a better story to hold on and abstain and wait and prepare our bodies and our minds for such a beautiful day of celebration. It makes the celebration that much sweeter. And besides, abstinence is never fatal. I know. It's been ten years and counting, so far, and I'm still alive. Lol.

More than a few of us are watching that old grandfather clock wind down as we become grandmothers ourselves. I've got another two, maybe three years left on this body before I lose the two good muscles still holding up without the help of Spanx. But my prayer to God for a husband is not just about the timing. I want to be in love again. I want to date and laugh and hear a baritone voice that doesn't belong to my son at the breakfast table. And I want to do it in a way that honors my body, my family, and my God.

I want my knight in shining armor with a heart like God's heart, broad shoulders, and eyes that see only me. I want a man who will pray with me, fast with me, and make me laugh. I want my happy-ending story.

And so here goes nothing, while I'm waiting for everything. Praise God!

Reflection—In the Strength of God

Relationships these days can be dizzying, especially when it comes to waiting through loneliness without compromising our faith. Psalm 27:14 tells us to take heart and to "wait on the Lord: be of good courage, and he shall strengthen thine heart: wait, I say, on the Lord" (KJV). Pause here and reflect on what has for you been the most difficult part of waiting. Are you ready to trust God with it?

An Offered Prayer

O Lord,

Teach me the sufficiency of your grace as I wait for you. Give me the understanding to know my value. Drown out the voice of loneliness in the strength of your love. Keep me, Father, from compromise. Keep me in integrity and in your love as I wait. I pray your strength be mine. Amen.

11

Why Do I Feel So Lonely?

Twitterpated

"For this reason a man will leave his father and mother and be united to his wife, and the two will become one flesh."

—Ephesians 5:31–32

Yes, being comfortable being single can be a struggle. The loneliness can be so much louder than the voice of righteousness. I know, because I almost blew it not so long ago. I almost did the very things I teach against. You know, moving too fast, not listening to God, wanting to have things my own way.

And so that you won't make the same mistakes I did, I want to share my testimony with you now. As you read, know that it's not a sad story. It's just another example of the many ways God rescues us from ourselves and how He really does know best.

It is my prayer that you will hear my heart in this chapter and find some nugget of wisdom or example of God's faithfulness that encourages your heart and blesses you.

Journal Entry—December 2001:

My darling . . . We should have been forever.
should have told you that I loved you when I had your ear and you had my heart
should have held your hand longer and ran slower when you chased me in the park
I should have laughed at your stupid jokes
should have watched wrestling or at least pretended
should have given you more cover for your feet and more love for your heart
I should have loved you better.

Back then, I was one of those people who fill life with things. I was not committed to God, so there was a God-void in my heart I wasn't even aware of. I spent so much time building a great career that I neglected to build relationships. Those who loved me endured me. Yet, there was a guy, a very special guy . . .

From the moment we met, I knew he was different from other men I had dated. He wasn't put off or intimidated by my corporate climb and strong persona. In fact, he encouraged it. My success was his success, and we did well together. Honestly, I never thought it would end, until it did. Michael Trinidad died in Tower One of the World Trade Center on September 11, 2001.

From that day, I barely spoke of him. After the terrorist attacks and my escape from Tower One, I felt very alone.

I struggled mentally, physically, financially, and spiritually. So much so that there was no room in my soul to deal with emotional issues. And as a result, it took a long time to be able to move on from such deep wounds.

Then I met God. And after I gave my heart to Him and my life to the lordship of Jesus Christ, things were okay. I began to breathe—first long deep breaths of relief. Then joy filled me. Hope enveloped me, and there were no voids or empty places in my life whatsoever. Like a sponge, I hungered for the knowledge of God: to learn His ways and to please Him. There was no greater joy in my life than being in His presence. In fact, I'm quite sure I never knew what love was until I embraced the Lord.

Although I accepted Him as my Lord and Savior in 2001, I officially entered into His service in October 2003. The minute I said yes, my life and ministry moved full speed ahead. I wrote books and traveled and spoke at churches and led church groups, and did everything I could to spread the message of hope to those who were broken, as I had been. And all praise to God, lives were impacted, and for the first time in my own life, I felt I had a purpose.

Meanwhile, years passed. Then one day, completely out of the blue, I reconnected with my childhood best friend. It was great. It was fast—only minutes from our first three-hour phone call to our first face-to-face visit, or so it seemed. Likewise was the introduction of her husband's childhood best friend to me.

He had a beautiful smile. He was bright, insightful, and loved God. He held a meaningful position in the church. He loved street ministry and children and even knew my family, so he said. It was meant to be, so it seemed. A whirlwind romance, so it felt.

Whatever it was, it had us spending hours on the phone and days traveling between New York and Chicago for visits. He called me every morning, just to say hello, and every night, just to "hear my voice." We were sharing secrets and aspirations and spending time with each other's families. We were having picnics and pizza and visiting family churches. Before I knew it, I was wearing a beautiful diamond ring of engagement.

I just knew it was God. All the signs were there. So when I found out he was divorced and had kids, I hesitated only a little. But I paused when my brother expressed his concerns over some things that had come to light. Red flags were thrown in the mix when my son told me he didn't like him at all. And what should have been the final nail in the coffin was my friend Tiffany's prophetic dream. Everybody who loved me had reservations.

But by then, the voice of loneliness was louder than the voice of the Holy Spirit. I kept thinking about all the cities I had visited alone, the airports filled with strangers, and my empty house. I needed to belong to someone, and more than anything, I just wanted a relationship with a man that was not complicated.

So I used Scripture about grace and forgiveness and love to support my own desires. I blew through relationship stop signs like a NASCAR driver.

Normally, I'm not the least bit impulsive. I'm not prone to silly behaviors or doing things that don't make sense. I'm the steady one—practical, focused, reliable. Not this time.

We were engaged just three months after we started dating. We set our wedding date for Valentine's Day. I bought my dress, reserved the church, the social club, and the honeymoon resort, got rid of my home in New York, and the invitations were on their way out the door.

Then two days before Christmas, when I was expecting him in New York, he called me from a New Mexico airport to tell me, "I don't love you, and I don't want to marry you." The End. No explanation. No remorse. No tenderness. Nothing.

In that one phone call, every insecurity I had ever believed about myself came rushing forward—every lie the enemy had ever told me about being difficult to love, or being crazy and high maintenance . . .

> The Lord is close to the brokenhearted and saves those who are crushed in spirit.
>
> —Psalm 34:18

My heart broke in a million pieces. I was so distraught I made myself physically ill.

Only God can take pain that huge and ease it. And not by wrapping His arms around us as humans do. He's too big for that—but by getting so near to us that He envelops us. He becomes for us a covering, a cocoon or nurturing layer that *is* strength. And the feel of His presence is so much more substantial than the feel of the pain; it is all encompassing. In His presence there is quiet.

My God, you are GREAT!! My heart rejoices in that!
Journal Entry—February 14, 2009:

"Sometimes I feel there's a hole inside of me, and emptiness that at times, seems to burn. I think that if you lifted my heart to your ears, you could hear the ocean, deep and wide. And the moon tonight is beautiful."[1]

*I have this dream of being the better half of some-
one, of not going to sleep every night wanting. But still,
sometimes, when the wind is warm and the crickets sing,
I dream of a love that God will give me and I pray for
him. Wherever you are on this earth, may God's love
keep you and my love be bread crumbs to your heart. I
just want to be someone's most important kiss. I don't
know . . . maybe I've had my happiness. I don't want
to believe it, but . . . well, there is no husband, just me
and the moon.*

Once again, I needed the mercy of God—broken, empty,
embarrassed. I wish I could tell you I handled it like a trooper.
But I didn't. I had a tantrum. I balled my fists at God, stomped
my feet, pounded on the floor, and cried for days. I vowed I
would never ever open myself up like that again.

Father knows best.

It was a year later when I learned my "ex" was not the man
I thought he was. It took me some time to get there and to
grow up a bit, but I was able to pray for him and for his family.
And it was not all his fault. I was moving much too fast from
the beginning. I was speeding up when I should have slowed
down. I was blowing through stop signs and ignoring that
"prickling" from the Holy Spirit of God that told me *no*. I
was talking to God when I should have been listening. And
even though all I really wanted was love and marriage, I was
following my own ways to have it (Proverbs 3:6).

So it's all good now. And I have experienced a whole new
gamut of living that only the gift of pain unveils—freedom
from the fears that close us in, release of insecurities that
hold us hostage, forgiveness of the bitter memories that keep

us bound to lies and love—unconditional, mature, and completely without self.

Pain—though it's the gift nobody wants—yields closeness with our Creator God that cannot be achieved by any other means. And it is *the* assurance that even though we only see it in hindsight, God's hand *will move* on our behalf. He is always near, especially when it comes to matters of the heart (Psalm 34:18). And we rejoice, resting in the peace that only comes in living through pain and in waiting.

Speaking of waiting, I sat down the other night and watched the movie *Bambi*. I love it. It is one of the most tear-jerking, beautiful coming-of-age stories of all time, even if it is a children's animated tale. As you may remember, the main characters are Bambi, a white-tailed deer, two dear friends, Thumper (a pink-nosed rabbit) and Flower (a skunk), and his childhood friend and future mate, Faline.

One of my favorite scenes is when Bambi, Thumper, and Flower are skipping about in the forest, sharing stories and exploring nature, when they notice two birds fluttering about and chasing each other.

> Flower: [*seeing the two birds*] Well! What's the matter with them?
>
> Thumper: Why are they acting that way?
>
> Friend Owl: Why, don't you know? They're twitterpated.
>
> Flower, Bambi, Thumper: Twitterpated?
>
> Friend Owl: Yes. Nearly everybody gets twitterpated in the springtime. For example: You're walking along, minding your own business.

You're looking neither to the left, nor to the right, when all of a sudden you run smack into a pretty face. Woo-woo! You begin to get weak in the knees. Your head's in a whirl. And then you feel light as a feather, and before you know it, you're walking on air. And then you know what? You're knocked for a loop, and you completely lose your head!

Thumper: Gosh, that's awful.

Flower: Gee whiz.

Bambi: Terrible!

Friend Owl: And that ain't all. It could happen to anyone, so you'd better be careful.

[*points at Bambi*]

Friend Owl: It could happen to you . . .

[*points at Thumper*]

Friend Owl: . . . or you, or even . . .

[*Flower looks at Owl shyly*]

Friend Owl: Yes, it could even happen to you!

Thumper: Well, it's not gonna happen to me.

Bambi: Me neither.

Flower: Me neither.

Leslie: *Me neither. Well, maybe . . . after all, spring is in the air.*

Reflection—God With Us

Loneliness and the distracting flashing lights of human fellowship are powerful adversaries to knowing and feeling God's presence. But no matter how lonely you might feel, God *is* with you. Our innate spiritual desire is to live in the presence of God, but our flesh will be prone to loneliness, and we cannot spiritualize our flesh. Think about how much time you are actually spending with God, absorbing the fragrance of His presence, which can overcome the feelings of being alone. Do you need to spend more time with God?

An Offered Prayer

Lord,

Only in your presence am I complete. Teach me to abide in you and to shuffle off these mortal habits. I look to you only, Lord, for deliverance from the pain of loneliness my flesh is prone to. Help me to hear your voice and not the voice of my own pain. Thank you, Lord, for calling me to call on you in this difficult time. Amen.

12

How Do I Know When to Let Go?

Hope Less, Believe More

"Let us hold unswervingly to the hope we profess, for he who promised is faithful."

—Hebrews 10:23

Perhaps this is your life. Until now, you may very well have lived in response to life—in a sort of passive mode—just you and your beating heart, waiting for the spectacular to happen. You've gone about your everyday, doing what's expected of you and being who you're expected to be. And except for a nagging sense of discontent, everything has been okay.

You have settled into a small group at church and done some mission work. You've taken classes and read books to better your life, but somehow beneath the surface of that

113

happy mask that still fits after all these years, your soul longs for more.

You have pressed on through layoffs, repossessions, and past-due bills, through loneliness and romantic dates that never happened. You've pressed on through sickness, weight gain, broken relationships, and the humdrum of the ordinary. You've managed to keep hoping things will get better.

And despite the odds, you're still believing that no matter how life looks or what anybody says, if you hold on long enough, everything is gonna be all right. Because deep down you're an optimist. You were taught to believe. And just like your parents and their parents before them, you're hanging in there with good old-fashioned, leg-slappin', hootin' and hollerin', rollickin', rampant, blind-as-a-bat hope.

And we all need that hope, don't we? Especially today, when the entire world is turned upside down, and what once was a light at the end of the tunnel has flickered. People are wracked with bitterness and despair, and real faith has been abandoned. Just walk through any school, government center, even some churches.

These days faith is weakened, hope is sparse, and people everywhere are either coming up short of it or holding on to the last tiny bit of it while praying for radical change in their lives. Desperate times have led to desperate measures.

And so now instead of allowing faith to be the substance that establishes our hope, we rely on hope to *manage* our faith. We hope our families will improve. We hope an argument will work itself out. Hope we don't have cancer. Hope to lose the weight. Hope to get married or have a wonderful marriage. Hope to be encouraged. The list goes on.

But hope is not a strategy, nor is it a plan.

We cannot just surrender our outcomes to a notion. Or, has hope become that audacious?

Too often when we are in distress, we reach for something to encourage us to hold on. But that something is often no more than wishful thinking—false hope. And false hope compels us to pursue objectives that have no ground in reality and happy endings that have no basis in truth. It keeps us holding on when we should be letting go—closing our eyes to reality, repeating the same mistakes over and over again, expecting different results. We claim our victories while ignoring the facts and never addressing the evidence. And we call it faith.

Yet if we put our hope in the wind, we will always, always be left wanting.

But where are our teachers to show us the difference?

Why do we still so inadequately discern the truth and live a life of faith that is beyond our circumstances? Shame on those whom God made to be our caregivers—apostles, prophets, evangelists, pastors, and teachers—who teach us to pretend a hope that does not deliver when our homes are but houses, our money buys medicine but not health, and our churches are just buildings and we find no solace there.

When our friends have their own troubles and can't be there for ours, when our personal pain is increased by the pain of our broken families, when our hearts are heavier than the burdens we carry, and our souls graduate from dismay into despair, woe to those who shift the truth by teaching words in Christ's name but not the Word of Christ.

Shame on political leaders who promise too much and spiritual leaders who promise too little. Shame on blind seers, carnal prophets, and pastors with no tears. They feed us sermons with no meat and delightful points of interest with no nutritional value. They give us biblical portraits of nothing at all and glances of revelation on this or that—all in the name of inspiring hope. They leave us wanting.

My God, my God, why hast thou forsaken us?

And what is out there, Lord, that is enough to satisfy a broken soul and mend a wounded heart? What is confident enough to look harsh reality in the face, give it its due, and command it to be changed? What is powerful enough, faithful enough, and colossal enough to keep standing through the toughest storms, break through the hardest hearts, and deliver life?

Enter the God of all comfort with the hope that faith is built on, established in Christ and based on His promises . . . not the wind. Enter the assurance that God will never leave us or forsake us, for we are more than conquerors through Him who loved us. Thank you, Jesus.

Enter the God who *causes* all things to work together for the good of those who love Him and are called according to His purpose (Romans 8:28), performing His great works and speaking life into His creation. Answering prayers, supplying our needs (Philippians 4:19), and asserting that our entire households will be saved (Acts 16:31). And as we wait, His grace is sufficient for us (2 Corinthians 12:9), He will uphold us through temptation (1 Corinthians 10:13), and "[He] is able to keep you from falling, and to present you faultless before the presence of his glory with exceeding joy" (Jude 24 KJV).

All praise to God, we *are* absolutely more than conquerors through Him. And our hearts are lifted. And joy is complete. And we have hope as we rely on His promises and the cares of this world are cast on Him, for He cares for us.

Through this, we hope less and believe more.

Reflection—Holding On vs. Letting Go

I don't have faith in faith or hope in hope. I believe in God, I have faith in His truth.

—Anonymous

Too often when we are in distress, false hope feels better than no hope at all. And so we are compelled to pursue objectives that have no ground in reality and happy endings that have no basis in truth. We keep holding on when we should be letting go—closing our eyes to reality, repeating the same mistakes over and over again, expecting different results. Are you holding on to things or people when you should be letting go?

An Offered Prayer

Father,

Give me today the wisdom to choose and trust the way of faith, no matter what. Uplift my spirit and encourage me in your promises and not my own way. Amen.

The Church and the World

I am afraid of a new wave of religion that has come. It started in the United States, and it is spreading. It is a sort of esoteric affair of the soul or the mind, and there are strange phenomena that attend it. I am afraid of anything that does not require purity of heart on the part of individuals and righteousness of conduct in life. I also long in the tender mercies of Christ that among us there may be the following:

A beautiful simplicity. I am wary of the artificialness and complexities of religion. I would like to see simplicity. Our Lord Jesus was one of the simplest men who ever lived. You could not involve Him in anything formal. He said what He had to say as beautifully and as naturally as a bird sings on the bough in the morning. That is what I would like to see restored to the churches. The opposite of that is artificiality and complexity.

A radiant Christian love. I want to see a restoration of a radiant Christian love so it will be impossible to find anyone who will speak unkindly or uncharitably about another or to another. This is carefully thought out and carefully prayed through. The devil would have a spasm. He would be so chagrined that he would sulk in his self-made hell for years. There should be a group of Christians with radiant love in this last worn-out dying period of the Christian dispensation, a people so loving that you could not get them to speak unkindly and you could not get them to speak uncharitably.[1]

—A. W. Tozer

A Puritan Prayer . . .

O Lord, in prayer I launch far out into the eternal world, and on that broad ocean my soul triumphs over all evils on the shores of mortality. Time, with its gay amusements and cruel disappointments never appears so inconsiderate as then. In prayer I see myself as nothing; I find my heart going after Thee with intensity, and long with vehement thirst to live to Thee. In prayer my soul inwardly exults with lively thoughts at what Thou art doing for Thy church, and I long that Thou shouldest get Thyself a great name from sinners returning to Zion. . . .

In prayer I place all my concerns in Thy hands, to be entirely at Thy disposal, having no will or interest of my own.

In prayer I can intercede for my friends, ministers, sinners, the church, Thy kingdom to come, with greatest freedom, ardent hopes, as a son to his father, as a lover to the beloved.

Help me to be all prayer and never to cease praying. Amen.[2]

13

As Christians, Aren't We Supposed to Prosper?

The Means or the End

"He shall be like a tree planted by the rivers of water, that brings forth its fruit in its season, whose leaf also shall not wither; and whatever he does shall prosper."

—Psalm 1:3 NKJV

I grew up in a home where God's goodness and holiness were among the first things Mom taught us. By her words and actions she demonstrated God's faithfulness to our family. And we were always reminded of the works of His hands. So if we knew nothing else, we knew God is holy and He alone should be loved, worshiped, and reverenced.

Over the years, my siblings and I have held on to that belief. Consequently, our eyes were opened and we witnessed His love in our lives on every level, and we loved Him back. In fact, every one of my brothers and sisters and their children are God-fearing, God-honoring born-again Christian believers. Our knowledge of and experiences with God keep us giving ourselves to Him daily.

So even after my time away from the church, I'll never forget the first time I heard a pastor say, "God is good." It took me back to those good old Bible-thumping lessons of my younger days. I was all aboard from there. But instead of hearing about coming to God because of His holiness, His grace, and His love for us, the pastor went on for almost an hour about "accepting" Christ because of the joy, peace, and prosperity that being a child of God brings.

How disappointing. But unfortunately that's the popular message today. Everybody's peddling Jesus for all that He's worth. "Say yes to the Lord and receive the abundant life." "You can have what you say." "Seek the kingdom first and God will give you everything you ever wanted." Everywhere we turn, slogans tell us to "Come to God and get what you want!" As long as you believe, you will never lack for anything again. Life will be blissful and happy and everything you need, from food to clothes, and everything else, from a big house to a nice car, will be given to you.

I'm not sure where the idea that being a Christian guarantees worldly bliss and prosperity came from, but I wish I could send it back in a blaze of fire and brimstone so the entire world could witness its demise.

Of all the distorted teachings within Christianity today, this so-called prosperity gospel and some teachings around the kingdom of God are probably the most detrimental to the life-blood of believers. And with some well-known evangelists and pastors holding their lives up as evidence of success, people now equate God's blessings with material things. They're out of balance and biting down hard on a doctrine that is only as deep as our pockets, believing that the blood of Jesus paid the price for our happiness. This quest for happiness, not Jesus, is so pervasive that Christendom is now seen by many as having only this end in view: God exists to please mankind, and the goal of faith is for mankind's benefit.

What about love? When did we stop loving God for who He is and start loving Him for what He can provide? When did the word get out that He is Jehovah-Jireh (the God who provides) and no more? Subliminally we are being trained in a pursuit of things rather than a pursuit of God. God is no longer the end goal; He is the means to the end goal.

And what about those who are lost? What guarantee of salvation will they ever find in securing a bigger home? What healing from cancer comes via large bank accounts and faster cars? The Word of God tells us that it profits nothing for a man to gain the world and lose His soul (Matthew 16:26).

Interestingly enough, the soul of man is not and will never be drawn to God by what He can give us. We are drawn by His love and kindness and what He saves us from (Romans 2:4). We don't need gimmicks or slogans or feel-good messages. That is not what John the Baptist taught. Nor is it what Peter or Paul or Billy Graham taught. These men combined have led millions to Christ with a message of repentance and grace.

There have been times when I stood before thousands with a message of hope and God's grace, and people came, kneeled at the altar in droves, and gave their lives to Christ. After being reminded of the goodness of God, people open up to Him. It feels good and right to know that God is concerned about the condition of our souls and the fulfillment of His purpose. Everything else is just everything else.

Personally, I find it hard to believe that the same God who, for His sake and ours, hid mysteries in himself in order to bring about a grand purpose that we can't even grasp, would place value in the square footage of our homes or the lot size of our property. This teaching is of no benefit. There is no spiritual value here whatsoever. It simply leads people into despair and even apostasy.

That's what happened to a man I met a few years ago who was living beneath the poverty level and was deeply depressed. He wasn't working, but he had an honest desire to improve his living conditions and to understand what God's Word said about his finances. He stumbled upon some kingdom studies and the prosperity gospel. When I say he was heavily immersed in it, that is an understatement. This man listened to recordings all day and proclaimed this doctrine. He did everything the evangelists and preachers instructed him to do, including fasting.

Three years later, he is still living in poverty and in a home with poorly working plumbing and no heat, wondering why God hasn't changed things for him. I have watched him sink into despair. He gets offended at any correction offered and refuses to share his true situation with believers who would help. He won't accept even the possibility that he is traveling the wrong road.

I have watched helplessly as this man wrestled between thinking his circumstances are the result of some super-duper demonic attack and the belief that he is poor because he is living outside God's will. He believes his faith should deliver him. But faith is not God. Faith is faith. And when our faith becomes god, it loses its power. Because the true and sovereign God says we shall have no other gods before Him (Exodus 20:3), even if it does resemble Him. Besides, as we read in Lamentations, "Who can speak and have it happen if the Lord has not decreed it? Is it not from the mouth of the Most High that both calamities and good things come?" (3:37–39).

God's will for our lives is not for our continual comfort. God's will for us is His eternal salvation and that His divine purpose be completed in us by any means necessary. And for some of us, that may mean a lack when it comes to material things.

Lack is uncomfortable, I know. But Jesus himself was poor and homeless. So was I. And so are many others whose lives are gloriously exciting and satisfied in every way. In fact, most of Jesus' most passionate and dedicated followers not only suffered throughout their lives, they experienced cruel deaths, as well. They were persecuted, stoned, tortured, imprisoned, slain by the sword, beheaded, fed to lions, crucified, burned alive, beaten with rods, and hated by many (Hebrews 11).

Both John the Baptist and Paul were beheaded. Simon Peter was crucified head-down, at his own request. Andrew, brother of Simon Peter, was crucified in a spread-eagle position; James, son of Zebedee, was beheaded—"put to death with the sword" (Acts 12:1–2). Philip, James, Jude, and Matthew were all martyred. Bartholomew met his death by being flayed, or skinned alive, and then beheaded, and Thomas was viciously speared to death.

Yet none of us would ever challenge the faith of these men or God's attentive ear to their prayers. Each of them is still held in high regard in heaven and on earth, known as faithful to God and dedicated to the gospel message of Jesus Christ toward the fulfillment of God's kingdom purpose.

And in reading through their stories, we see that even in their most extreme sufferings and lack, not one of them "spoke" to their situation, prayed for abundant provision, or strived to be anything or anywhere other than in the station where God had placed them.

Paul wrote, "I know what it is to be in need, and I know what it is to have plenty. I have learned the secret of being content in any and every situation, whether well fed or hungry, whether living in plenty or in want" (Philippians 4:12). And the psalmist added, "My comfort in my suffering is this: Your promise preserves my life" (Psalm 119:50).

So then, why do we expect to live differently today? How can we believe that things in God's true kingdom have changed—especially if God is immutable (Hebrews 13:8)? Why do we believe that we should never be hungry or lack anything? Why do we assume that sickness or struggle is a sign of little faith and a life lived outside of the will of God?

God forgive us, because I think we still believe the lie that was believed in the garden: that God is withholding good things from us. Despite His faithfulness to us throughout the generations and despite the promises of eternity, despite who He is in His divine nature, we still hold on to the thought that perhaps there is something out there that is bigger than God and we have a right to it.

But "Who is God besides the Lord? And who is the Rock except our God? It is God who arms me with strength and keeps my way secure. He makes my feet like the feet of a deer; he causes me to stand on the heights" (2 Samuel 22:32–34). He is God, and he is worthy that we should give to Him all the glory, all the honor, and all the praise, just as Shadrach, Meshach, and Abednego did (Daniel 3–4).

Their love for God was fresh and committed, so much so that they refused to compromise and serve the gods of Babylon. Before being thrown into the fiery furnace as punishment, the king gave them one last chance to change their minds, but they declared, "If we are thrown into the blazing furnace, the God we serve is able to deliver us. . . . But even if he does not, we want you to know, Your Majesty, that we will not serve your gods" (3:17–18). They were willing to give their lives for the love of God, and they were willing to accept God's will for them no matter what it was.

What amazing love and commitment, to be in a place within ourselves where we can affirm that even if God does not meet our expectations, even if He does not grant our happiness, even if He does not prosper us materially, we won't compromise to false doctrine or worship according to the "come and get it" gospel. It honors God when we love Him with all our hearts and souls and minds. We will worship God and exalt His name, but not because of what He does for us or what He gives, but because of who He is. You see, God must always be sought for himself alone, never as a means toward something else.

This morning, when I was reading A. W. Tozer's *Man: The Dwelling Place of God,* I came across something so perfectly suited for this chapter that it would be a shame to exclude it. Take it in.

Loving God Only

The first and greatest commandment is to love God with every power of our entire being. Where love like that exists, there can be no place for a second object. Yet popular Christianity has as one of its most effective talking points the idea that God exists to help people to get ahead in this world! The God of the poor has become the God of an affluent society. We hear that Christ no longer refuses to be a judge or a divider between money-hungry brothers. He can now be persuaded to assist the brother that has accepted Him to get the better of the brother who has not! Whoever seeks God as a means toward desired ends will not find God. God will not be one of many treasures. His mercy and grace are infinite and His patient understanding is beyond measure, but He will not aid men in selfish striving after personal gain. If we love God as much as we should, surely we cannot dream of a loved object beyond Him which He might help us to obtain![1]

Reflection—Prosperity of the Soul

My close friend and senior advisor, Avor, always says, "Jesus came to the earth to die for souls alone. He couldn't care less about your stuff." And she is right; God's promise of prosperity refers to the condition of the soul, not our riches, as many believe. If we seek His kingdom riches, which are all about fruitful living and gifts of service, there is no lack in life because there is no lack in Him. How prosperous is your life right now?

An Offered Prayer

Lord,

There is great pressure in society to live and collect a lot of stuff. Consistently we seek you to find easier ways to get more and be more, and we call that prosperity. Forgive us, Father, and teach us your ways. We've been deceived by the enemy to continue to pray for our own needs, when we have everything we can possibly imagine. Help us, Father, to heed the words of Jesus and take no thought as to what we will eat or drink or what we will wear, and to instead focus our prayers on the nations and the health of our souls. Give us confidence that you know every one of our needs. Open our eyes to the truth and cause our hearts to accept it . . . according to your will, let it be so. Amen.

14

If God Is In Control, Why Does Everything Seem So Out of Control?

"I AM"

"And we know that in all things God works for the good of those who love him, who have been called according to his purpose."

—Romans 8:28

No others words were so perfectly suited to close the previous chapter than those of A. W. Tozer. He is one of my favorites to read. I love his voice and the expression of his honest heart toward God. I find that as a writer he had a gift of capturing and articulating the depths of man's heart.

I'd like to share with you more of his thoughts on the sovereignty of God:

Who wouldst not fear Thee, O Lord God of Hosts, most high and most terrible? For Thou art Lord alone. Thou hast made heaven and the heaven of heavens, the earth and all things that are therein, and in Thy hand is the soul of every living thing. Thou sittest king upon the flood; yea, Thou sittest king forever. Thou art a great king over all the earth. Thou art clothed with strength; honor and majesty are before Thee. Amen.[1]

I sit in amazement at God's awesomeness. As I meditate on His Word and who He really is, my mind follows His light. And it compels me to a place that is higher than my human ability to understand and I tremble in a biblically terrible awe of God. There are no words. It brings me to my knees. "Elohim Gadol."

Throughout history, mankind has wondered about the existence of God. We have wrestled with the complexity of His sovereignty and tried to understand why bad things happen to good people. And when it comes to explaining such things as natural disasters, evil, and suffering, many Christians opt for the explanation that God is all-powerful and all-good.

But the world won't acquiesce. There is just too much complexity in life to accept such simplistic reasoning. So in-depth teaching has come from good seminars and anointed pulpits offering "God is in control" as the answer. It's how we've managed complexity.

And so now, deeply rooted in our Christian subculture and permeating our logic is the idea that the simple explanation "God is in control" is all we need. It's become the favorite, the shoe-in, the catch-all phrase when our theology fails us and we need to explain disaster, murder, rape, and a miserably failed economy to a seeking soul. And many gifted theologians are on board with that approach.

In his book *The Sovereignty of God,* evangelist and biblical scholar A. W. Pink wrote, "God foreordains everything which comes to pass. . . . God initiates all things, regulates all things."[2] Edwin H. Palmer took Pink's position even further: "God is in back of everything. He decides and causes all things to happen that do happen. . . . He has foreordained everything 'after the counsel of his will' (Ephesians 1:11): the moving of a finger . . . the mistake of a typist—even sin."[3]

While I think these thoughts have some substance, they lack the whole truth. I'm not sure how we got off track, or when the phrase "God is in control" invaded our vernacular, but offer it up to a holocaust or 9/11 survivor, or use Pink's or Palmer's theology when talking to the mother of a child who has been brutally raped and sold into slavery or the father of a son tortured and then butchered at the hands of a madman in the Middle East, and take note at what comes back at you. People need more than words.

People are broken and in pain. They are disappointed and despondent, and we, the church, are offering them fool's gold. You see, following a teaching like that and offering it as a means of comfort does not bring peace to the brokenhearted. It brings anger and resentment. The idea that God is somehow sitting on the outside of our lives playing the puppet master and causing evil things to take place in our lives is not only unbiblical, it's insane. Moreover, it sets up true followers of Jesus Christ to ridicule.

Atheists, agnostics, and nonbelievers mock us and constantly challenge our faith, and rightly so. For if God really is in control, they say, why doesn't He stop suffering? If He

133

can and doesn't, He's a monster. If He can't, He isn't an omnipotent God who can save us.

Think about it. Either we believe in a God who is truly sovereign, or we don't, and we make excuses for Him. I think as believers, questioning God's control is something we are afraid to do out loud because we fear its implications—if God really isn't in control, then the world is a lot scarier than we ever imagined. And if things can happen outside of Him, then there is no point to our salvation or our suffering and Jesus died for nothing.

To tell you the truth, I've wrestled with this theology for a long time. And while I can quite easily agree that God is all-powerful and that nothing moves or has its being without His will, I cannot agree that He instigates immorality, because in Him there is no guile. And here's the part we miss.

The conflict is not in God's sovereignty or His control. The conflict or problem is in our thinking. We are confusing God's control with His sovereignty. We're starting from the middle of all things, when, as Paul did, our study of God should start from the beginning, with God, before time.

Walk with me. The English word *sovereignty* is defined as independent power. But in early Hebrew teachings, sovereignty has no definition; it refers to God's identity. So in ancient Scripture, when referring to God's autonomy, the prefix *aleph* is used. The aleph expresses the free-will act of God whereby He, according to His supreme authority and will, created man, distinct from Him yet still dependent on Him. Free will is an attribute God has given to His reasoning creation.

Hence, all power originated from one place: God. Nothing— not power or principalities or heaven or earth—was created outside of Him, that is to say, separate from His being. We know from the book of Revelation that the angel Lucifer, a reasoning creation, corrupted a portion of that power in himself when he rebelled against God. That was the birth of evil. So while God does not cause evil, evil—before it was evil—came from God. And in the same way that nothing can be good without God, no evil exists without Him either.

I know this is going to be a challenge for some to grasp, but God's sovereignty is about His supreme authority over all that He has made, not the subjugation of it. He will maintain His universe, choose to bring judgment to the earth, and He will offer us His plan of salvation. His control is about giving His reasoning creation the power to make genuine, independent choices. This is the free will to act.

In His sovereignty, God delegated a final destiny for this world in two paths. Under His control, He has given to us the freedom to choose which path we will take. We decide our own fate. We make our own mistakes and live with the consequences. And that's what's going on in the world today. We're living the consequences of choices.

The decisions we have made, including the abandonment of faith, have created an abysmal world by our own free will to act in whatever way we choose. We are getting out of life what we have put into it (Galatians 6:7).

So when we question why children suffer, the answer is, we aren't taking care of them. When we ask why there is so much poverty in the world, it's because we're selfish and don't share our wealth. When we wonder why life is so out of control, it's because we are.

And while not everything happens in the world in exactly the way God desires, nothing happens without His acquiescence.

God permits the sadness and pain of life to press upon us the consequences of sin, and sometimes we'll even live the consequences of someone else's sin or recklessness.

Galatians 6:7–8 tells us not to be deceived: "God cannot be mocked. A man reaps what he sows. Whoever sows to please their flesh, from the flesh will reap destruction; whoever sows to please the Spirit, from the Spirit will reap eternal life." Like my daddy would say, that's not the exception; it's the rule.

The loss of the *Titanic* was due to careless racing through an ice field. The tragedy of September 11, 2001, was due to deviant and evil madmen with delusions of a religious war and hatred for everything American. Both of these tragedies affected thousands. Neither was an act of God. Both were acts that God allowed.

Yet God is still our Redeemer. He still meets us in every situation at the place of our need, hears the cries our bleeding hearts fling at him, and bears with us when in misdirected anger and pride we stomp our feet and shake our fists at Him, questioning His control. He still listens even when we deny His love and challenge His existence. By an act of His own will, He loves us with an undying love. And in His sovereignty *and* in His control, He causes the best of things and even the worst of things to weave together for our good (Romans 8:28) and eternal life with Him. That is His promise. That is His Word. That is His sovereignty.

And so after all has been said and done, I'd have to agree, that yes, indeed, God is in control!

Reflection—Praying With Confidence

There is a great big world out there that God is caring for. No matter how big it feels, our lives are brilliantly intertwined in all of it. We are one piece of a huge master plan and conglomeration of things. Romans 8:28 lets us know that God works together all those things for a greater end goal. In other words, He causes all things. By His hand, He moves things on our behalf so that we have the full confidence in *knowing* that He is ever present and ever active in His universe and in our lives. God does not observe our lives happening from the sidelines. Therefore, when tragedy touches a believer, we should understand that God will bring some good from it for us and around us. This is the greater good. So think about it: Until the world is restored, all of us must suffer at times for the greater good. How comfortable are you with that, or are you still praying for a life outside of His control?

An Offered Prayer

Father God,

Help me to be assured and confident in your unseen power at work in me and around me. Amen.

15

If God Is Sovereign, What Is the Point of Praying?

The God of Possibilities

"Do not be anxious about anything, but in every situation, by prayer and petition, with thanksgiving, present your requests to God. And the peace of God, which transcends all understanding, will guard your hearts and your minds in Christ Jesus. Finally, brothers and sisters, whatever is true, whatever is noble, whatever is right, whatever is pure, whatever is lovely, whatever is admirable—if anything is excellent or praiseworthy— think about such things. Whatever you have learned or received or heard from me, or seen in me—put it into practice. And the God of peace will be with you."

—Philippians 4:6–9

I sat on my bedroom floor with my back against the side of my bed—almost like a 1960s sit-in; head back, legs crossed, arms resting on my knees . . . the whole works. My eyes were low and dim from crying all night because once again I was faced with my own mortality—a large lump in my left breast.

As many times as I've been here, you'd think I'd be more graceful in my approach to God and His throne. Instead, I was kicking and screaming and feeling as if I'd just had the wind knocked out of me . . . again.

I had lived quietly with this lump for months, resting my head on God's shoulder like a kid, and wrestling with whether to pray for healing or assume that my present state was by God's own hand. Eventually I decided to pray for healing. My plan was to impress God by being high-minded in my request, saying all the right things and quoting Him in all the right Scripture, making it impossible for Him not to give me exactly what I wanted.

I asked the Lord that if it was for the greater good of everyone invested in my life to remove the lump, that He do it right then, without the assistance of surgery. I reminded Him of how much I love Him and how much I really want to be with Him. I said, "Lord, cancer is not my first choice as an exit strategy from this earth"—now, if that hadn't touched His heart. . . . Then I just talked and talked and talked to Him—about my new friends and the return of a very special old friend, about life in general, and the things that matter most to me, like Eliot's salvation.

A few nights later, after coming in from a brisk five-mile run, feeling exhilarated and very healthy, I decided to check for the lump. To my surprise, instead of one lump, there were two. I pressed my hand against my chest in disbelief.

Suddenly, tears that were about to flow were interrupted by a laugh from my belly as the Holy Spirit unexpectedly filled me with His joy. I'm not sure why or how I found this so funny, but I have to tell y'all, it was the most incredible experience I've had in a long time. Experiencing the peace of God was all-consuming. Somehow, I knew way down in my knower that my prayer had indeed affected God, and despite my current situation, all was well.

I know. That must read like I'm a deep and spiritually grounded woman of faith, who easily accepts everything life offers. Truth is, most times I'm simply comfortable enough in my own skin to reveal my whole heart to Him despite my kicking and screaming. I realize it might be a challenge to see God in situations like that. But to know God is to know that we are indeed in His care and under His control. It again points to His sovereignty and what He allows in our life experience.

There really is no reason for us struggle with it . . . ever.

For some of us, however, the default position is to ascribe suffering to failure. Our tendency is to believe that only circumstances that bring us ease show God's favor, and challenging circumstances are not of God at all. But as the writer of Lamentations asks, "Is it not from the mouth of the Most High that both calamities and good things come?" (3:38).

Even our earthly father's table gives us both fruit that we like and vegetables that we don't like. So if God really is our Father, and He is, then this makes perfect sense. It means that when we pray, God hears us and liberally involves himself in our lives, causing both the good and what is perceived to be not-so-good to *collectively* feed us.

Prayer is the connection that He uses to do that. Without that connection, prayer is a vague, disjointed, and at its best, an impersonal "task" on our checklist of good Christian things to do to make God happy.

But when we connect, our prayers reach past our understanding and beyond the constraints of time to bring about the perfected vision that God has for each of us.

For example, from my childhood and throughout my teenage years, I would often hear my mother on the phone with her prayer partner praying for me and for each of my sisters and brothers. Her voice was melodious, always steady and filled with compassion. One could almost hear the tears of brokenness and love sweetly pass over her lips as her words, wet and absolute, resonated throughout our home and upward toward heaven. One by one she'd call our names and beg God to save us.

I loved hearing my mommy pray!

She is with the Lord today. But here we are, more than forty years later, and as I said earlier, every one of my mother's children and her children's children are born-again, spirit-filled believers! Her legacy to us is her faith and how she prayed.

I thank God for my mother's prayers! I thank Him that He instilled in my mother a consistent uprightness, and that the prayers of the upright accomplish much—even from generation to generation! Psalm 37:25 says, "I was young and now I am old, yet I have never seen the righteous forsaken or their children begging bread." And James 5:16 reminds us that "the effective, fervent prayer of a righteous man avails much" (NKJV).

Hallelujah to the Lamb of God! There is more power in that kind of prayer, by that kind of person, than there is in anything else on this earth, below it or above it, because it moves the hand of Almighty God.

Understand that when we pray in earnest, prayer is so much more than a one-sided means of communicating with

God. It is *the* intimate connection by which we give ourselves wholly to Him. And God, choosing to walk with us in covenant, generously gives us insight into His nature and charge over our outcomes—not in *response* to our prayers, but in *provision* of our prayers.

You see, a response is always a reaction to something. And God does not react. There is never any new information for Him to consider in our circumstances. In all things He is the initiator—even when we pray.

That's the key. And the implications of that are mind-blowing! Think of it. It means that God is the starting point to all that we ask. And being so, He, before the official life clock started, accounted for every one of our requests. Charles Spurgeon explained it this way: "God is always first. He is before our convictions, before our desires, before our fears, and before our hopes."

Once again, you might be thinking that all is truly great in the land of Leslie Haskin, where the Holy Spirit provides constant revelation only to her. The truth is, I too am ever learning. I teach best what I need most to learn.

It wasn't so long ago that I prayed and fasted relentlessly and with full, childlike faith for my godson—a struggling heroin addict—to be delivered. It was a crushing blow when he died in a car accident in what we believe was a drug-induced rage.

I unreservedly trust God today and have moved on from that particular incident and many other disappointments in my life, but in my younger years as a believer I needed all the things of God to fit neatly in a little box marked *spiritual*. I struggled to resist pessimism in the face of seemingly unanswered prayers. I struggled to let go. I struggled with accepting the fact that spiritual things are spiritually discerned, and some things will never be ours to know. There are still times I struggle to make human sense of God's sovereignty and His immutability in line with how He answers prayer.

I know that because God instructed us to "pray in everything" (Philippians 4:6), then everything is capable of being shaped by prayer. The big questions for me were: If prayer changes things, what exactly does it change? And if God is sovereign, which He is, why pray at all?

I read and researched and questioned God and became so intensely focused on intellectualizing God's "methodology" that I almost lost sight of Him. Then once again, and as He always does, God showed me mercy. He slowed me down enough for me to become reacquainted with another old friend whose own faith in God's delight of our prayers reminded me of my mother's.

I was reminded of all that I've seen over the years.

I've witnessed incredible obstacles moved from the path of God's children. I've seen lives changed at His hand. I've been in places where miraculous healings took place right before my eyes and agnostics declared my God to be the one true God. I have prayed and afterward experienced miracles with my finances, my friends, and even my health.

Time and again the prayers of the people of God have brought victory. Time and again, when God's people bowed their wills to Him in prayer (2 Chronicles 7:14), no difficult family member or hopeless condition, no desperate circumstance or illness have remained a mountain.

And in my witness to all that, I realize now that God is bigger than our understanding (Isaiah 55:8–9). His ways are not our ways. What He does is outside the scope of any human intellect. And my little cranium or yours will never fully wrap itself around our connectedness to God and His willingness to be affected by our prayers.

From minute details to immense possibilities, God remains faithful in that He has *already* provided for us through prayer! He had already provided for Moses when He placed the sea where it was—and opened it up at the appropriate time. He had already provided for Deborah when He made the mountain slope at the place where it did, and then brought the rain at the appropriate time for battle. He had already provided for my mother in placing in her the incredible faith that kept her on her knees for each of her children, and then saved us across the generations.

God has an excellent track record of *always* getting it right! He is in front of our prayers, showing the way to deliverance or salvation or whatever we need, even before we pray. Again, He is the beginning and the initiator. It is He who calls to us and we respond to His call in prayer—mind-boggling, I know.

So why pray? We pray because God has moved our hearts to do so. Prayer moves the hand of God in our loves and our lives in line with His will. And how does God answer our prayers? He has gone before us. Long before time was, God did all we ever need Him to do. He has already said what needs to be spoken. So what does it matter how He does it? He does it!

We get in our cars every day and drive here and there without really understanding the ins and outs of the engine and the drive shaft. We walk into our homes and trust they won't fall down around us, without in-depth knowledge of beams and load-bearing walls. We breathe without holding our breath to first figure out all the whys and how of lungs and oxygen and staying alive.

Why can't we do the same in prayer? Why can't we just open our minds up to God, praying with thanksgiving and knowing that He already has!

Prayer honors God because God honors prayer.

Jesus called Lazarus from the dead in a simple three-word prayer. Jesus stepped out on the water with no words spoken. He did not tell His Father how to make it happen or figure out what properties in water could be considered solid. He just believed and stepped out. And the waters held Him up.

Hmmm. I think the simplest explanation of how it all works comes again from my experiences with my mother. When she made a pronouncement in our home and we asked her why, she'd just say, "'cause I said so." I believe prayer is God's way of saying, 'cause I said so.

So why not just pray *and believe* without first requiring an understanding of all the dynamics and how God makes it all work? Why not simply step out or call out? Why not just accept the only explanation that we really need, which is: It works because God said so.

Let's pray.

Father,

We come now to you, expecting a connection. You are all we seek.

Our hearts are filled with love and with passion for you. You have put within us a hunger and thirst to know you more, and so as we enter this moment, we do so with great expectation that you have met us here, and that being in your presence, the eyes of our hearts will be opened wide to receive your truth.

Father, we know that in your presence, bodies are healed, broken dreams are restored, and lives are transformed . . . because you said so. Now consume us. Change us, and send us forth from here knowing the kind of selfless faith that will manifest your love throughout our families and those we love, so that no matter the circumstance, they will come to know you . . . because you said so. Amen.

Reflection—The Prayer of Faith

We should not pray only to get something out of God. Our prayers should be to bring something out of us as well.

The Hebrew word for prayer is *tefilah*. It is derived from the root *Pe-Lamed-Lamed* and the word *l'hitpalel*, meaning to judge oneself. This surprising word origin provides insight into the purpose of prayer. The most important part of prayer—whether it is a prayer of petition, of thanksgiving, of praise to God, or of confession—is the introspection it provides when we look inside ourselves to see our role in the universe and our relationship to God. When we do this, it takes the focus off things and puts it on us. We then learn to be confident with God managing the details and causing them to work out. Are you the type of person who needs to be in control of everything? If so, be honest, does that mean you don't trust God?

An Offered Prayer

Thank you, Father, for all things.

16

Is Hell Real?

The Reality of Eternity . . . Under Fire!

"And if it seem evil unto you to serve the Lord, choose you this day whom ye will serve; whether the gods which your fathers served that were on the other side of the flood, or the gods of the Amorites, in whose land ye dwell: but as for me and my house, we will serve the Lord."

—Joshua 24:15 KJV

The whole system works, from beginning to end—the plan for our salvation and the remission of our sins, communication with God and fellowship while here on earth, using our gifts to serve God and His people, fighting the good fight of faith, and finally living out God's purpose and our reward in eternal glory with God our Father and Jesus Christ our Lord. Hallelujah!

It really doesn't get any better than that.

And this is the beauty of life, that "God so loved the world that he gave his one and only Son, that whoever believes in him shall not perish but have eternal life" (John 3:16). From the end to the beginning, God has revealed His plans and His purpose for us. Those who accept Him as Savior and Lord will reap the rewards, and those who don't will reap as well. The bottom line is eternal death vs. eternal life: "For the wages of sin is death, but the gift of God is eternal life in Christ Jesus our Lord" (Romans 6:23).

And there is no hotter topic right now than eternity. Thanks to a firestorm ignited by a few well-known pastors who question hell's existence, more people than ever are engaging in conversations about heaven and hell.

While no one objects to the idea of going to a "better place" after we die, mention hell and the tone changes. The implication that there could be an eternal fire as sentence for sin sends people up in arms, cursing God and denying Him.

For skeptics and Christians alike, hell causes big problems.

And here's where the serpent speaks and the questions behind the questions come to the surface: How can a loving God send people to hell?

Journalist Lee Strobel, in *The Case for Faith,* interviewed Talbot School of Theology philosophy professor J. P. Moreland about the topic of hell. He basically said that what the Bible is teaching about hell is not literal. Moreland said, "Hell *is* punishment—but it's not punish*ing*. It's not torture. The punishment of hell is separation from God, bringing shame, anguish, and regret."[1]

He went on to offer an explanation that because we will have both body and soul in the resurrected state, the misery people will experience in hell will be both mental and physical, but not a physical experience of burning.

Well, that's a nice clean picture, isn't it? Add a couple of beverages and a few friends and he's got himself a nice party. But there is one problem with it. It's a lie—and if we bite into it, there will be irrevocable and horrifying consequences.

The Bible tells us very plainly what hell is. In the book of Matthew, Jesus describes it as a place of outer darkness (Matthew 8:12); a furnace of fire where there will be wailing and gnashing of teeth (Matthew 13:42); and everlasting punishment (Matthew 25:46). Reading further in Luke 16:24, a man cries, "I am in agony in this fire." And there are even more vivid descriptions by John in Revelation: the bottomless pit (9:1 KJV); a gigantic furnace (9:2); no relief day or night (14:11); the fiery lake of burning sulfur; and the second death (21:8).

It sounds ruthless. So I totally understand the push to imagine a more palatable place, because to admit its reality is to also face the possibility that it could one day become our own.

Several years ago I read *Beyond Death's Door* by Dr. Maurice Rawlings, a specialist in internal medicine and cardiovascular disease. Dr. Rawlings retells the details of many situations in which he helped resuscitate people after they were declared clinically dead. He recorded the details in his book. Until a certain incident in 1977, Dr. Rawlings was an atheist, who, in his words, "considered all religion 'hocus-pocus' and death nothing more than a painless extinction."

In 1977, Dr. Rawlings was resuscitating a man who, terrified and screaming on the table, was begging for help. Rawlings wrote:

> Each time he regained a heartbeat and respiration, the patient screamed, "I am in hell!" He was terrified and pleaded with me to help him. I was scared to death. . . . Then I noticed a genuinely alarmed look on his face. He had a terrified look worse than the expression seen in death! This patient had a grotesque grimace expressing sheer horror! His pupils were dilated, and he was perspiring and trembling—he looked as if his hair was "on end."
>
> Then still another strange thing happened. He said, "Don't you understand? I am in hell. . . . Don't let me go back to hell!" . . . The man was serious, and it finally occurred to me that he was indeed in trouble. He was in a panic like I had never seen before.[2]

Dr. Rawlings wrote that no one who heard the man's screams and saw the look of terror on his face could doubt for a single minute that he was actually in a place called hell.

But many people do doubt the reality of hell. And what we believe is our decision to make. God has given us the free will to act and to choose our fate. So if you don't like the idea of hell, it's simple; you don't have to go there. It's like going to McDonald's to eat and verbally attacking the servers because there is no pizza on the menu. In Christ's death and resurrection, God offers an alternative: life. The Word says, "For God so loved the world that he gave his one and only Son, that whoever believes in him shall not perish but have eternal life" (John 3:16).

Belief in Jesus Christ is a point of acceptance, not proof. And acceptance of Him is a matter of choice, not obligation.

Last week I was pulled into a conversation with a very intelligent young woman who was visiting a dear friend of mine. The woman, I'll call her Sally, was an atheist, who knew a little about my testimony about Jesus Christ and was ready to "prove me wrong."

Over coffee, Sally told me she did not believe in "my God" and that if there is a hell, it is right here on earth.

Picture this: I am sitting at a large country-style kitchen table near a window. My legs are crossed at the ankles and I'm leaning in to my cup to carefully sip the steaming brew. When Sally made her statement, I paused, my cup stopped less than an inch from my lips, my eyes rolled up over the cup's rim, and in my best diva-liscious voice I said, "Good luck with that."

My dismissive response must have shocked her a bit, but after a brief pause she told me the many reasons that I and millions of other Christians are fools. She said it makes no sense that finite sins are infinitely punished.

I calmly offered an explanation.

God gave us a list of things not to do in order to protect us from the consequences. That's what sin is. And those who say a loving God should prevent the sin need to acknowledge that that is exactly what the Bible seeks to do. So if we choose to disobey, we should get what we ask for. No one escapes the consequences of his or her own choices.

We can be sure that one day that little girl who was taken from her bed in the middle of the night, raped, tortured, and savaged, will be vindicated when the evil that devoured her is cast into the lake of fire (Romans 12:19). Peter wrote that God is patient with us because he doesn't want anyone to perish (2 Peter 3:9). But someday, Peter continues, God's patience will run out and "the day of the Lord will come like a thief" (v. 10). Every person will get in eternity what they bought here on earth (Romans 6:23).

For the most part, I just let Sally talk, interrupting only to ask pointed questions, which stirred up more and more passionate responses in her. It wasn't long before she was up and walking around the kitchen, waving her hands in the air and stomping her left foot at times. She clearly believed everything she was saying.

I just smiled, which caused her to ask why.

I paused for dramatic effect, and replied, "So I think I hear you saying we were all born in hell?"

"No!" she yelled in frustration. "You're trying to be funny."

"No," I said. "I'm not. I'm just trying to make sure I understand your point. If hell is right here and now on earth, then we were all born in hell. So out of curiosity, I'd like to know what the alternative is. And since the concept of hell itself is actually mentioned in the Bible, that must mean you believe the Bible. And if you believe the Bible a source reliable enough that you believe hell exists, why does it become unreliable in its description of it?"

The conversation ended when I told her that she had my permission to believe and to live however she chose. I respected that, but in return, I requested her permission that I do the same.

You see, as someone truly in love with the Savior, I'm not interested in proving God is not a liar. Nor am I interested in the apologetics and the firestorms that constantly swirl about Him. Our conversations about God should not seek to prove His existence or His love. They are simple facts.

Unbelievers show up time and again wanting to "save Christians" from the foolishness of God and the Bible. They are in our faces constantly, saying they don't have to believe in our Jesus. True, but why do they have to keep talking about a Jesus they don't believe in? The problem is not with their not believing, the problem is their attacks on what I believe.

No other walk of faith is criticized and hated as much as a true Christian's walk. It's globally okay to speak about God in general, or Muhammad, or Emma, and even Buddha. But mention Jesus Christ, and you're next in line to be crucified. Churches are burned. Christian books are protested, and even prayer pages on Facebook are defiled, all in the name of freedom to believe. As Christians, don't we get those same freedoms?

Tell me something, friends, why are true followers of Jesus Christ expected to tiptoe around nonbelievers while they walk all over us?

I'm done keeping quiet and playing nice because someone might be offended by my words. I've sat at my last table with the last pleasant smile on my face while people call my God a liar. My life was saved by the Christ they hate, and I will not stand idly by anymore.

I get it, this is not about condemnation, and our battle is not with flesh and blood. Salvation is a gift to be freely received. Even amid debate and righteous indignation, God doesn't *need* any of us to come to His defense. But that's what love does.

We should willingly put on the full armor of God every day and take up the weapons of warfare to defend the one we love, to fight the good fight, committed to our Father. We are born-again, Holy Spirit-filled believers and followers of Jesus Christ, not doormats. And like it or not, this is war—a war like all wars, that will at its end have those who triumph and those who do not.

What's at stake here is a lot more than being right.

Reflection—Finding God in an Encounter With Him

The vague and tenuous hope that God is too kind to punish the ungodly has become a deadly opiate for the consciences of millions.

—A. W. Tozer

Frankly, the saddest and most fierce component to life is the reality of hell. Too often we forget to mention it or we shy away from the subject because it's so uncomfortable for us to talk about. But how comfortable do you think it will be for those who make it their eternity? Have you shared the full gospel message today? Have you compelled someone to come to Christ?

An Offered Prayer

Holy Father,

Thank you for sending your Son, Jesus Christ, to pay the penalty for our sins. See my heart of gratitude, Lord, and give me the courage to speak it freely to others. Give me courage to remind them of the gift of salvation and the punishment for sin. In my discomfort about hell, remind me of the flames that devour and the certainty of those flames for those who do not accept Christ. In this, compel my mouth to speak boldly the truth without fear of offense, but in love and determination to win souls for the kingdom of heaven. Break my heart for the things that break yours. In Jesus' name. Amen.

17

Is Jesus Really the Only Way to Get to Heaven?

One Way

"When I say to the wicked, 'You wicked person, you will surely die,' and you do not speak out to dissuade them from their ways, that wicked person will die for their sin, and I will hold you accountable for their blood."

—Ezekiel 33:8–9

Eternity—that's what life is all about. It's not a simple dispute over what hell will be like. It's a critical choice regarding who will go there.

Our world has become so senseless in so many ways that we miss the point of having these conversations in the first place. As born-again Christians, our dictate is to spread the gospel and make disciples of nonbelievers. We should not get roped into proving or disproving heaven and hell. As I've said, spiritual things are spiritually discerned, and I am confident that God will, by His Holy Spirit, bring light to a seeking soul who really desires to know the truth.

Jesus Christ made an enormous and passionate sacrifice so that no one would have to go to hell. You see, hell was not intended to be a means of punishment for us. It was a place for the devil and his angels (Matthew 25:41) to be eternally punished and separated from us, so that they would do no more harm. But if we choose to join them in their wrongdoing, we also must join them in their punishment. Although God has planned a way for us to avoid this death, He will not stand in the way of our own free choice.

We offer Christ. We pray that the eyes of the unbeliever would be opened—even in a world of blindness. "God so loved the world that he gave his one and only Son, that whoever believes in him shall not perish but have eternal life" (John 3:16).

And having paid so great a price, the world still rejects Him. It disregards His divinity and pushes moral tolerance as the highest virtue so that the idea that truth is relative to one's own experience is widespread. In our present society, the accepted culture has God dethroned and regarded as a mere higher power. And so it is considered outrageous to claim that Jesus is the one and only exclusive way for people to get to heaven.

I've seen staunch believers sidestep the issue. I've seen arguments break out and lives threatened all because Jesus said He loved us and gave His life to prove it. Shouldn't that be a good thing?

Instead, wars are fought. Thousands are killed. Families break up and churches are burned to the ground, all because Jesus said, "I am the way and the truth and the life. No one [man, woman, boy or girl] comes to the Father except through me" (John 14:6).

And I believe Him. That's what Scripture teaches, and that's what I believe. And once upon a time that's what the true church believed and taught as well.

In the late '60s and '70s, society was very morally aware. How people behaved, how they measured success, and so on, was still very much tied to biblical teachings. The life question then was "How does God expect us to live?" There was no mention of the "god that is me." The gospel message was still the "good news," and there was even a campaign for truth called the Jesus Movement.

It was huge. And it was given credibility and momentum by scores of evangelical groups that boldly rejected modern-day teachings and boldly declared that Jesus Christ is the only way to heaven. Their very cool "One Way" sign—an index finger, held high—became the popular icon and slogan. There were One Way bumper stickers, T-shirts, lapel pins, posters, cups, and cards everywhere. The movement was loud, in your face, and broadly respected and accepted. There were even community movements that led people to Christ. There was very little if any debate that Jesus was indeed the only way.

So what changed?

Modern times have birthed ego-driven ministries and the disappearance of God. Small congregation shepherding and fire and brimstone preaching are things of the past. In their desire to be relevant, fashionable, and seeker-friendly, many church leaders have adulterated the gospel message—the one thing that gives us an understanding of our worth and ignites passion in our souls. As we become more steeped in tolerance, we move further away from speaking the hard gospel truth. In Matthew 10:34, Christ said, "Do not suppose that I have come to bring peace to the earth." Jesus is speaking about a message that divides like a sword. It is the division of truth from error, and the reaction of the darkness against the light. Some will listen and accept it, but many will violently reject it. And although we will be hated for the message of repentance that we bring, we are still required to bring it.

Still, many of our churches avoid repentance and preach only a feel-good gospel. They don't teach about heaven and hell anymore. They don't teach that the Bible is the one truth. They shy away from bold messages that preach that you must be born again, and their songs of praise are often just well-orchestrated, well-timed noise.

For their own vainglory, some build for themselves churches with a priority to fill the pews without consideration for filling heaven. They desecrate the pulpit with sermons of prosperity over holiness, the embrace of secular music over sacred, and altar calls are a thing of the past. This is not the church that God told us to build.

In 1 Corinthians 12, Paul describes God's intention for His church—the body of Christ. It is made up of believers, not a mere building. Yet as we visit many churches today, we find many are boldly and definitely out of order, tradition having replaced the Word of God (Mark 4:19). And the cares of this world, and the deceitfulness of riches, and the lust for other things have entered in and made us unfruitful.

The Bible says, "In vain they worship Me, teaching as doctrines the commandments of men" (Matthew 15:9 NKJV). In Mark's parallel account of this statement (NKJV), Jesus says, "All too well you reject the commandment of God, that you may keep your tradition" (7:9). Then Jesus said (v. 13), "making the word of God of no effect."

What have we become when our churches are in danger of God's judgment and some of our pastors are leading them there?

When I was a little girl, I remember sitting in the front pew at church. Most times it was because I was in trouble and the ushers had to keep an eye on me. But other times, I sat with Mom and actually listened to the message that was being preached. I loved hearing the melodic baritone voice of the preacher, his hands raised to God, crying for people to repent and be born again.

But that was back in the day when church was church. I loved everything about it. The ushers decked out in white uniform dresses, white stockings, and white shoes, pointing people to available seating with white-gloved hands. The choir proceeded from the back of the church to the sound of the opening hymn. The deacons stood in the front during the entire service, and the elders actually kneeled and prayed for the presence of the Holy Spirit to rain down on us. (I actually watched for that rain.)

We had weekend shuts-ins of nothing but fasting and prayer. And the prayers were so intense that one couldn't deny the presence of God. We passed out gospel tracts in our communities, had youth meetings, held membership drives, laid hands on the sick, and actually saw miracles happen "in the name of Jesus."

What happened to us?

Perhaps the church as a whole has compromised its backbone, and the enemy of our souls is devouring our promise of eternity, one church at a time. The devil is stealing our willingness to be black-and-white about the tenets of the faith and instead is creating among us various shades of gray.

Our judgment is distorted, and what once was forbidden is now perfectly acceptable. What was once universally deemed immoral is now championed as lifestyle preferences. We are giving in to the idea that marital infidelity and divorce are okay. Profanity is everyday language. Abortion, homosexuality, and other sexual and moral perversions are regarded as freedom of choice by large advocacy groups and enthusiastically promoted by the popular media. This whole silly notion of moral tolerance is steadily turning genuine morals and biblical doctrine upside down, while we who are to blame claim to be blameless and stand idly by in shameful silence . . . until we have no more voice.

We have lost our credibility, and the world rejects our claim to know the truth. Under the weight of New Age philosophies and confused evangelicals, society has turned away from the Bible and ultimately from God, saying Christianity's claim that there is but one truth and that Jesus Christ is the only way to heaven is unproven and lacking in authority.

While many are drinking the many-ways-to-heaven Kool-Aid, I have taken up the sword that Christ has given to me. And no matter the amount of popularity or lack thereof in my position, I am deeply committed to living a life of radical integrity and grace. And while I am all in favor of transparency, authenticity, and respecting differences, I don't believe in religious tolerance. The whole concept makes me cringe.

As I see it, it all boils down to yet another deception of the serpent, who once again has engaged us in the same old garden conversation: "Surely God did not say to you that Jesus is the *only* way?" And unfortunately not much has changed in us. On some level, we still want to be God. We still want to choose our own lifestyles and our own eternity, with no thought of consequence or righteous judgment.

But like it or not, God alone declares our end. According to the law that He has established, He alone will announce our eternity, and without doubt we will come face-to-face with three absolute truths. Hell is not an idea, it's a place. Salvation is not a concept, it's life. And Jesus Christ is not an option for getting to heaven, He is the only way.

To my church and my friends, hear my heart. This is more than just another chapter in a book. This is a matter of life or death. There are no do-overs.

If I have described your church here, get a few people together and pray for the move of God's hand in your church. If I have described you here, pray for the move of God's hand in you.

If you truly love God and believe in His Word, I challenge you to raise your voice with the truth. Take up the sword that Jesus Christ has given to us. Stop living in silence and playing church while the world dies of brokenness and lies. If only one person hears your voice and takes heed, imagine the possibilities.

So whether you are moved to anger, annoyance, or tears, it's okay, as long as you are moved to change. We can't afford to be intimidated by the devil into softening the bold claims of Jesus Christ and widening that narrow road. If we do, we are in trouble. One day, the blood of those we passed by will be required of us (Ezekiel 33:8–9).

Whether the masses accept us or not, we must go boldly with the truth that one day our lives will end. And every one of us will stand face-to-face before the living God to give an account of our lives.

We will stand before an Almighty God, and He will assign to each of us our place in eternity. We will look at His face and know this truth: Indeed there are many roads that lead us to Him, but only *one* that will keep us there!

Be encouraged!

Reflection—Eternity Means Forever

We can't afford to be intimidated by the devil into softening the bold claims that Jesus Christ is the only way to God. One day, the blood of those we lied to will be required at our hands. Ezekiel 33:8–9 says, "When I say to the wicked, 'You wicked person, you will surely die,' and you do not speak out to dissuade them from their ways, that wicked person will die for their sin, and I will hold you accountable for their blood. But if you do warn the wicked person to turn from their ways and they do not do so, they will die for their sin, though you yourself will be saved."

Whether others accept our word or not, we must boldly tell them the truth that one day life will come to an end. And every one of us will come face-to-face with the living God, who will require an accounting of our lives. What have you done for Him lately?

An Offered Prayer

Savior,

How majestic is your name in all the earth! Thank you for creating me, remembering me, and taking care of me. Thank you for declaring my worth on the cross and providing the way to an eternity in the presence of my Father. Help me to help others know this truth. In Jesus' name. Amen.

18

Why Aren't We Believers Doing Greater Things Than Jesus Did?

Now, That's a Good Question

"Believe me when I say that I am in the Father and the Father is in me; or at least believe on the evidence of the works themselves. Very truly I tell you, whoever believes in me will do the works I have been doing, and they will do even greater things than these, because I am going to the Father."

—John 14:11–12

Throughout history, mankind has always been preoccupied with certain questions. Who are we and how did we get here? What is our destiny? Why were we created? These questions continue to confound even the most brilliant minds in the fields of science, medicine, and theology. Devout and learned believers suggest that God created humankind because He desired a relationship with us, close communion, and worship.

But it seems to me irreverent somehow to suggest that God *needs* any of those things. God is completely autonomous, self-directed, and sovereign. And while it's one thing to say He created humankind because He is a God of love (1 John 4:8), it's quite another to suggest He created us because of a need to receive love. God's love is intrinsic to His nature, as is intimacy and companionship. And regarding His glory or His magnificence, He is not vain or in need of validation from anything or anyone. He is God.

Have we still not grasped the sheer enormity and other-worldliness of Him? Are we still struggling to wrap our minds around the fact that God is too big to be reasonable to our understanding? You see, in order for anything to have the capacity for explanation or reason, the object being explained must first be understood. There has to first be discovery. And God is much too *ginormous* to fit inside our small boxes of discovery. It's like the unborn fetus explaining the womb.

The apostle Paul tried to explain it in his speech at Athens: "The God who made the world and everything in it is the Lord of heaven and earth and does not live in temples built by human hands. And he is not served by human hands, as if he needed anything. Rather, he himself gives everyone life and breath and everything else" (Acts 17:24–25).

In other words, God existed long before we did. He is Creator of all things. And in no way does our existence validate His. Neither our belief nor disbelief in Him, or our understanding or lack thereof in Him changes the fact that our lives depend on Him and not the other way around—but again, why?

Why did He create us? Whether it is nobler to accept that there are some things we are not privy to or to press in for a richer glimpse of God's reasoning, and in so doing resolve our own, remains one of the simplest and yet most profound questions ever asked.

But I think our tendency is toward complexity. I think we make things more complicated than they need to be, and in so doing, we overlook this simple truth: The knowledge of some things in life indisputably belongs to God and we have no access to it whatsoever.

Since before the world began, God hid in himself a mystery that contained His purpose for Christ as well as the part of humanity that would accept Christ: the church. That which He purposed in himself, He would bring about after the counsel of His own will, according to His own good pleasure. This purpose would be extended to the church by grace alone in a way that was consistent with what He wanted.

In his letter to the church at Corinth, Paul writes, "However, we speak wisdom among those who are mature, yet not the wisdom of this age, nor of the rulers of this age, who are coming to nothing. But we speak the wisdom of God in a mystery, the hidden wisdom which God ordained before the ages for our glory, which none of the rulers of this age knew; for had they known, they would not have crucified the Lord of glory" (1 Corinthians 2:6–8).

We indeed were created for a specific purpose that is solely found in Jesus Christ. His life, the miracles He performed, His teachings, and His death reveal our purpose: to establish and carry on God's kingdom.

Let me explain. In His final message to His disciples, called the Great Commission, Jesus spelled out our life's goal. In His words we glimpse our creation purpose:

All authority in heaven and on earth has been given to me. Therefore go and make disciples of all nations, baptizing them in the name of the Father and of the Son and of the Holy Spirit, and teaching them to obey everything I have commanded you. And surely I am with you always, to the very end of the age.

—Matthew 28:16–20

In John 14:1–4, He said,

Do not let your hearts be troubled. You believe in God; believe also in me. My Father's house has many rooms; if that were not so, would I have told you that I am going there to prepare a place for you? And if I go and prepare a place for you, I will come back and take you to be with me that you also may be where I am. You know the way to the place where I am going.

Then Thomas said to him, "Lord, we don't know where you are going, so how can we know the way?"

Jesus answered him, "I am the way and the truth and the life. No one comes to the Father except through me. If you really know me, you will know my Father as well. From now on, you do know him and have seen him."

Then Philip jumped in with "Lord, show us the Father and that will be enough for us."

Jesus answered:

Don't you know me, Philip, even after I have been among you such a long time? Anyone who has seen me has seen the Father. How can you say, "Show us the Father"? Don't you believe that I am in the Father, and that the Father is in me? The words I say to you I do not speak on my own authority. Rather, it is the Father, living in me, who is doing his work. Believe me when I say that I am in the Father and the Father is in me; or at least believe on the evidence of the works themselves. Very truly I tell you, *whoever believes in me will do the works I have been doing, and they will do even greater things than these, because I am going to the Father* (emphasis added).

But what are the greater works that Jesus talked about?

If we take the world's view, these works are defined or explained from a self-centered place that looks for the spectacular and the sensational. It seeks to satisfy the flesh by "doing more" than Jesus did, performing more healings, delivering more people, and preaching more sermons. It becomes about works and achievement and earning something and trying to take back what was stolen from us rather than receiving what has been given to us: a royal priesthood.

It's from this earthly perspective that we ask, "Why aren't we doing more than Jesus did?" And that same perspective limits us to doing all the good works in the world in the name of *ourselves,* and that amounts to nothing at all.

But from the right side of the cross—the spiritual perspective—we cry, *Abba.* Motivated by His love and His divine purpose, we say, "Here I am, Lord, send me." And as we are going into all the world as He commanded, side by side and in perfect partnership with the Holy Spirit of God to "loose the chains of injustice and untie the cords of the yoke, to set the oppressed free and break every yoke . . . to share [our] food with the hungry and to provide the poor wanderer with shelter—when we see the naked, to clothe them, and not to turn away from [our] own flesh and blood" (Isaiah 58: 6–7), then the glory of the Lord is revealed and His name is greatly praised.

And so now consider this: Perhaps the "greater works" we will do are not about works or miracles or prayers or any "act of service." For which one of us will ever do anything greater than the one act of love or service that Jesus Christ did in the six hours that He hung from that rugged wood?

Perhaps these "greater works" are not actual works we can put our hands to. Maybe they cannot be counted or compared.

I submit to you that these greater things must be set in the context of the kingdom of God and interpreted as done through God's grace and by the One, Christ, who lives in us and through us. Just as Christ has become for us wisdom from God—that is, our righteousness, holiness, and our redemption—He has also become the means by which we accomplish "greater things." Perhaps these *things* are spiritual and immeasurable by human standards. These *things* are of a godly purpose and to an appointed and divine end to which we are not privy. These things add up to bringing about a divine plan that God himself put in place even before He uttered that single word: *light*.

Until then, we're living in the in-between—from the right side of the cross, which is not of this world. We are doing as Jesus did, traveling the roads of nations and spreading the life-giving message of a kingdom that is not of this world. We are bearing fruit, and by His Holy Spirit we are healing the sick, raising the dead, giving sight to the blind, and setting the captives free—for there is no nobler cause.

Reflection—Unfinished Work

I find that most times I am not doing the greater work, but I myself am the greater work to be done!

What about you?

An Offered Prayer

Holy Father,

I come to you by the authority of your Son, Jesus, who ushers me into your presence. Complete your work in me and your purpose for mankind. I pray that you will use me in ways I never dreamed possible, for your glory, and that you receive the praise in all I do. In the name of our Lord Jesus. Amen.

19

What in the World Is Goin' On?

It's About Time

"But about that day or hour no one knows, not even the angels in heaven, nor the Son, but only the Father. As it was in the days of Noah, so it will be at the coming of the Son of Man. For in the days before the flood, people were eating and drinking, marrying and giving in marriage, up to the day Noah entered the ark; and they knew nothing about what would happen until the flood came and took them all away. That is how it will be at the coming of the Son of Man. Two men will be in the field; one will be taken and the other left. Two women will be grinding with a hand mill; one will be taken and the other left. Therefore keep watch, because you do not know on what day your Lord will come."

—Matthew 24:36–42

D oes it seem like the world is unraveling? All over the globe, people are beginning to feel it, especially now that the global economic machine is grinding and screeching like a missed shift on a manual transmission engine. Even America is feeling the pinch.

Because our nation is one of the world's leading economic powers, we are usually one of the last to see the unraveling that the rest of the world experiences. And yet we find ourselves in that same garage, looking up and scratching our heads. *What in the world is going on?*

I believe we are living in the last days, and what is going on in the world is the preparation for the rapture of born-again Christian believers. At the risk of being repetitive, there are truckloads of signs: unemployment at an all-time high, the divorce rate in America at 50 percent, unprecedented erratic weather scenarios across the globe, worldwide food riots and shortages, economic deterioration, crimes against humanity, and a loss of governmental authority.

Things once taking place in the shadows have been brought to the light on a large scale. Things like abuse, sex trafficking, and even slavery. Did you know that more people are now being held in slavery around the world than at any other time? A 2008 documentary, *Call and Response,* reported that 27 million people are being held as slaves; 70 percent are female, nearly 50 percent are children.

Devalued human life and poverty are the forces behind many of these atrocities. It is believed that more than $32 billion is spent every year in human trafficking, and in India, children cost less than cattle.

Signs of the times?

Though the church has initiated talks about the end times before, with the present condition of things, many people are finally listening.

People are beginning to see that never before in history have the signs been so perfectly aligned together with apostasy. Never before have we suffered such great loss to the body of Christ, and people are calling out to God. The Bible lays it out in clear detail.

Men Will Love Themselves More Than They Love God

Above all, you must understand that in the last days scoffers will come, scoffing and following their own evil desires. They will say, "Where is this 'coming' he promised? Ever since our ancestors died, everything goes on as it has since the beginning of creation."

—2 Peter 3:3–4

But mark this: There will be terrible times in the last days. People will be lovers of themselves, lovers of money, boastful, proud, abusive, disobedient to their parents, ungrateful, unholy, without love, unforgiving, slanderous, without self-control, brutal, not lovers of the good, treacherous, rash, conceited, lovers of pleasure rather than lovers of God—having a form of godliness but denying its power. Have nothing to do with such people.

—2 Timothy 3:1–5

"Your gold and silver are corroded. Their corrosion will testify against you and eat your flesh like fire. You have hoarded wealth in the last days" (James 5:3).

Peter, Timothy, and James all describe what the world will be like in the last days, and there is no debating the similarity to what we are experiencing today. While Timothy writes about unsafe times and of self-centered people who have a form of godliness but deny the power of God, Peter describes people making fun of Christians; James speaks of irrelevant riches being gathered.

The last days are godless times. Scripture makes it clear that people of the end times will have no love for God, for others, or for anything good. And there's more.

Travel Knowledge Will Increase

Daniel 12:4 says, "But you, Daniel, roll up and seal the words of the scroll until the time of the end. Many will go here and there to increase knowledge."

In this Scripture, God gives Daniel two signs that will help us identify "the time of the end."

First, the ability to travel from one place to another would be unlike anything seen before. And knowledge would increase at a rate—and to a point—unlike any other time in history.

As we all know, until almost the twentieth century, the speed that man could travel remained fairly constant. We were limited to travel by foot, horse, and boat. Over the years we have graduated to automobiles, trains, and planes that can take us from one side of the earth to the other in hours.

No generation before us was able to leave earth and land on the moon, travel to one side of the world and back in a day, and have a (digital) face-to-face visit with as many family and friends as desired without ever getting out of bed.

We have graduated from smoke signals to iPhones, WebEx, and Skype.

While the primary application of "knowledge increased" refers to people understanding the prophecies of the book of Daniel, many theologians believe this prophecy also applies to an increasing knowledge of science, medicine, travel, and technology. You've probably heard reports about how the sum total of man's knowledge is doubling at a rate unlike anything in the history of mankind.

We are definitely living in the Information Age, when even the most skeptical mind must admit that knowledge is exploding in all directions. Medicinal cures are expanding; we're even beginning to clone animals. Science is advancing beyond what we ever imagined, and it is said that 80 percent of the world's total knowledge has been brought forth in the last decade, and 90 percent of all the scientists who have ever lived are alive today. Computers can process more than 1 billion instructions in a single second.

A portion of the book of Daniel was not to be understood "until the time of the end." At the time of the end, many would run to and fro through the Scriptures, comparing text with text, and understand these prophecies. We have reached that time.

And as the progression of signs increase, so does the intensity of them.

Increase of War and Death (Wars and Rumors of More Wars)

Jesus warned that as we approach the end times there would be "wars and rumors of wars" (Matthew 24:6) and that "nation will rise against nation, and kingdom against kingdom" (v. 7). And so it has been. Over the last few generations, we have seen an increased appetite for blood and violence, and wars have escalated. If we go back to the sixteenth and seventeenth centuries, when the gunpowder revolution was evident, it's easier to see that as we get closer to the end, depending on your point of view, we either become more sophisticated in the development of weapons or our resistance to them and their power decays.

The twentieth century was the bloodiest in history, starting with World War I, which sent millions to fight and die. World War II involved similar numbers and produced atomic bombs. We contended with Stalin and Hitler's death camps and wars in Korea and Vietnam.

Our generation has continued the bloodlust, with geopolitical situations all mixed up in a virtual cauldron waiting to boil over.

> And when he had opened the second seal, I heard the second living creature say, Come and see. And there went out another horse that was red: and power was given to him that sat thereon to take peace from the earth, and that they should kill one another: and there was given unto him a great sword.
>
> —Revelation 6:3–4 KJV

If we take a step back, we can see a gradual removal of moral peace from the world. We now have thermonuclear bombs, chemical bombs, germ warfare, and intercontinental ballistic missiles that can reach anywhere in the world in fifteen minutes or less. Ezekiel 38:22 says, "With pestilence and with blood I will enter into judgment with him; and I will rain on him and on his troops, and on the many peoples who are with him, a torrential rain, with hailstones, fire and brimstone" (NASB).

And it all comes together in the great falling away.

A Great Apostasy

We know that in the last days there will be many who will leave the Christian faith. The Great Apostasy, as it is called, is perhaps the most subtle of all end-times prophecies. We are already so far down the road of compromise with our tolerance gospel and our corporate governance of "ministry"—where funds are more valuable than people—that it is now safe to say, "We never saw it coming."

So clever is the evil one that he has deceived us into over-simplifying the signs of things to come in a way that we would surely miss the cues. According to his outline, the signs of the apostasy are (1) the world in political and economic crisis; (2) the Middle East conflicts; (3) the rapture; (4) the rise of the Antichrist and the mark of the beast; and finally (5) the new world order.

But it's not that simple. The end times have so many associated events, that, unless specified by the Bible, putting them in checklist order is enigmatic at best. I think a lot of subtle changes are already happening that will prepare us for what is to come. We are already being psychologically conditioned toward anti-Christian beliefs and a new anti-Christian worldview.

And what does that look like?

The Bible paints a pretty good picture of what the world will be like post-rapture. We see an atheistic government with no influence from religion—one that views religion as the cause of all the world's problems. There will be no private property, so that no one person is more privileged than anyone else. The government will control what is done medically, what is taught in schools, and even direct scientific endeavors. The book of Amos says people will suffer, look for God, and not find Him:

> Behold, the days come, saith the Lord God, that I will send a famine in the land, not a famine of bread, nor a thirst for water, but of hearing the words of the Lord: And they shall wander from sea to sea, and from the north even to the east, they shall run to and fro to seek the word of the Lord, and shall not find it. In that day shall the fair virgins and young men faint for thirst.
>
> —8:11–13 KJV

The writing is already on the wall. Over the past fifty years, we have slowly pushed the Holy Spirit of God out of our schools, out of our homes, and out of our lives. We have slowly but surely exchanged God's uncompromising gospel for a belief system that teaches tolerance of sin and iniquity, without even realizing that the transition was taking place. Terms like *politically correct* and *socially acceptable* are training us to embrace what society deems okay. We are being conditioned to think that homosexuality is born into the soul and that Jesus Christ is not the only way to heaven. Traditional religious beliefs are labeled extremist and radical.

Laws once based on absolutes are moving toward the nebulous, and science, with or without ethics and morals, is claiming truth regarding creation. Our schools have discarded a fact-based system of thought in favor of a feeling-based one, and teach non-absolute values, where history is open to interpretation.

And where is the church body in all of this?

Diminished. What once was a strong body, steadfast in the "One Way," is slowly weakening, compromising, and dividing. Fearful of being offensive and unpopular, longing for the world's acceptance, the church has succumbed to the pressure to be open-minded. Further destroying our credibility, weakening our voice, and undermining our power to influence the world (Matthew 12:25), we mock our own, criticize the human frailties of our leaders, and ostracize those who speak boldly for Christ.

For example, not long ago, Harold Camping said the rapture of the church would take place on May 21, 2011. He got the world's attention, and it was the perfect stage to introduce the truth. But everybody laughed, and as he got more attention, he also got more criticism from the church. We took what should have been our opportunity to speak life to a dying world to defame our own. The world hated Camping, and the church had its stones ready.

Whether we are looking at the spiritual and social conditions in the world or the boiling political cauldron of the Middle East, the rise of China as a superpower, the emergence of the European superstate, or the dissipation of resources in America, it would be naïve to expect smooth sailing from here on.

To survive this time of apostasy, the people of God must ignore the threats and rumors and choose instead to hold fast to God and His promises. We must rightly divide the Word of truth and stand strong in faith in this critical hour. "Let no one deceive you by any means; for that Day will not come unless the falling away comes first, and the man of sin is revealed, the son of perdition" (2 Thessalonians 2:3 NKJV).

There will be more terror and more death, more financial distress and job loss, more divorce and immorality, more depression, more sorrows, and more pressure to leave the Christ we know and conform to the new notion of "tolerance." And these things must be for the end to come for they signal the beginning of birth pangs (Matthew 24:8 NASB).

And as the onion layers continue to be peeled back and we see greater levels of detail about the coming time of distress, we must learn in these last days to discern the difference between truth and error.

Until Christ comes for His church, our lives will only make sense through the light of His sacrifice. In the meantime, I offer you this: Stand firm through the chaos and do not compromise. Look past your enemy and see the many ways that God is at work in our world, our towns, and in our lives.

We are living in between the times. But Jesus has come and lived as one of us. He died and rose again for all of us, and one day the kingdom of God, which was His message, will come as He has promised. Focus on His promises to you and *know* that He is not a man that He should lie.

One day, in the end, heaven will come to earth and peace will reign.

Look for it. Work for it! Point people to it! Stay faithful in it, for "The Lord is good, a strong hold in the day of trouble; and he knoweth them that trust in him" (Nahum 1:7 KJV).

Reflection—Sign of the Times

Our world today is ever-changing and rapidly getting worse. On a personal level, though we may be experiencing bankruptcy, foreclosures, depression, abuse, divorce, and so much more, our job is not to pray against end-times prophecy, but to pray for its fulfillment. It is a glorious end that we will see one day. Just hang in there! Ours is the glorious hope of His coming. Why should we be afraid?

An Offered Prayer

Faithful Father,

Your eyes see more than the world combined will ever see. So you know these days are rough and trying for us. Thank you for your heart of mercy and gentleness toward us. Thank you that you are not constrained by the economy. You can do ALL things beyond even this. And so I pray that you will encourage people who are suffering today. Send strong believers to their side to be a comfort for them and a listening ear. Even so, come Lord Jesus. Amen.

20

So, How Am I Supposed to Live a Christian Life With So Much Going on Around Me?

... Just Being Me

"May these words of my mouth and this meditation of my heart be pleasing in your sight, Lord, my Rock and my Redeemer."

—Psalm 19:14

I travel a lot to speak to groups. And normally my friend Shannon, who is very social, is with me to manage the social part of my trips. She's good at it and I'm not. In fact, I'm an introvert.

It took years before I was comfortable enough in my own skin to say no to birthday party invitations and social gatherings and crafting dates without feeling guilty. And it took an equal amount of time for my new Christian friends to accept the fact that the Leslie they saw in front of congregations and audiences is the limited-edition Leslie. She wears me out! I get my strength and energy from being alone. I absolutely need downtime.

Who is the total me? I am the complete package of God's gifts, skills, and physicality. That's the introverted speaker and lover of mankind. That part of me will never change. But my character—the sum of all my experiences, my learning and my external feeds, which fill up my soul or inner man, as the Bible calls it—can change. That's the part of me that talks to my friends nicely, or yells. LOL.

The third chapter of Ephesians describes the inner man as the part of us that God sees and judges—the combination of everything we put into our hearts via our mind. It's the place where sin happens.

We've all heard the expressions "You are what you eat" and "Garbage in is garbage out." Well, the same is true for our hearts. We are what we put into ourselves. If your heart is filled with good things, you will tend to think on good things. If your heart is filled with bad things, you will naturally think about bad things.

The music we listen to, what we read, television programs, conversations—these and other things, whether positive or negative, feed our brain and shape our character; how we treat people, how we spend our talents, how we think, what we think, what we value and pursue, and what we believe all have an effect.

Piece by piece, like adding bricks to make a building, we construct our lives with external sources. The question is, are we building our life into Frankenstein's monster or are we feeding our minds with Scripture, praise music, and gospel messages to help us in our Christian life?

I believe we are experiencing a crisis of carnality in Christianity today, so much so that many do not even recognize the person in the mirror. We are so caught up in societal influences and the desire to be accepted that we have lost sight of what godly behavior should look like. We follow the world's view and persistently live lives to please and serve self rather than to please and serve Christ. I believe much of what is wrong in our lives is attributable jointly to the condition of our thought lives and of our hearts.

But all is not lost. God has designed a perfect system whereby we can be holy in an unholy world! He invites us to pattern our lives after His. Though it can be a challenge at times, it *is* possible to avoid being affected by the ungodly influences of society and reject the world's view.

How? By being careful and changing what we "eat"—what we think about.

I read something a while ago that has stayed with me:

> Watch your thoughts; they become words.
> Watch your words; they become actions.
> Watch your actions; they become habits.
> Watch your habits; they become character.
> Watch your character; it becomes your destiny.
> —Author Unknown

We are children of God and have been called to something better. We are told to live lives of true purity, and this purity must start from the inside out. Christians are a peculiar people. But *peculiar* doesn't only mean "strange," it also means "chosen, selected, and unique." God has selected us for great and marvelous works, chosen out of the world, and thankfully, though He knows the present condition of our hearts, He sees the future health of our hearts as well. His ear is open to the heart's prayer and His desire is to heal our inner pains, change us from the inside out, and transform us into the vision that He had for our lives when He first gave us breath.

So there is no need to hide from God! There is no need to pretend. When we say one thing with our mouth and another with our heart, we lie to God—and it's pointless, because God ignores our words and hears our heart. And the heart cannot lie.

I think that's why our lives are so out of whack. We try to convince ourselves and God that we are something we are not. Most of us have learned how to mask who we really are and how we really feel about things. We have learned to pray as we think we ought to pray, and do what we think we should be doing for the greater good, but our hearts are distant from our actions.

Paul talks about that inconsistency. He says,

> If I speak in the tongues of men or of angels, but do not have love, I am only a resounding gong or a clanging cymbal. If I have the gift of prophecy and can fathom all mysteries and all knowledge, and if I have a faith that can move mountains, but do not have love, I am nothing. If I give all I possess to the poor and give over my body to hardship that I may boast, but do not have love, I gain nothing.

> —1 Corinthians 13:1–3

Jesus, on the other hand, took an extreme view of the fight against sin:

> If your right eye causes you to stumble, gouge it out and throw it away. It is better for you to lose one part of your

body than for your whole body to be thrown into hell. And if your right hand causes you to sin, cut it off and throw it away. It is better for you to lose one part of your body than for your whole body to go into hell.

—Matthew 5:29–30

When I was in therapy years ago, my doctor taught me to how to change my thoughts to keep my mind clear. Next I learned to meditate on God and His Word. The more I practiced, the more I realized that most of my thoughts were not biblical. They didn't follow the Word of God. They were in fact contrary. My thoughts would affect my heart, which produced actions that resulted in anxiety attacks. The panic attack I had when my son, Eliot, didn't answer his phone right away was following the lead of my heart, triggered by some bizarre television show or something else I had fed on.

I learned to catch negative thoughts and exchange them for positive, life-affirming ones. "Let this mind be in you which was also in Christ Jesus" (Philippians 2:5 NKJV). When I found myself dwelling on something undesirable, I began to renounce it and cast it away, even saying it out loud.

Sometimes, I imagined throwing it to the ground and stepping on it to kill it. Other times I imagined giving it to God in a box. In both scenarios, however, the end result was my getting rid of the thought and immediately replacing it with a good one, such as a prayer, a memorized Scripture, or a song.

I firmly believe that through God's grace and the power of His Holy Spirit, as well as the prayers and ministry of our brothers and sisters in Christ, we can reshape our character through a pure thought life. In doing this, our actions change. We will start to see changes in our attitude and behavior and eventually our world. Our hearts become pure and we are holy, even as Christ has commanded us to be holy.

So how do we do that? I'm glad you asked. Here's the hard part: We must say no to the craziness in our lives. We have to live on purpose and be proactive about what we allow in. As difficult as it might be, we have to break away from toxic relationships, avoid watching television shows that suggest ungodly behavior is acceptable, stop reading material that glorifies ungodliness, avoid pornography in all forms, stop indulging in conversations filled with cussing, refuse to listen to dirty jokes and gossip, and stop listening to music that promotes sin and ungodliness.

Instead of filling our minds with garbage, let's fill it with good things. Be diligent in the study and memorization of Scripture. Attend Christian events, read books that are morally correct and uplifting, listen to music that is edifying to the soul. (Jazz is good.) Form friendships with people who are positive, community-focused, and love and respect God. Give yourself permission to be wrong; don't criticize yourself or others seek the truth in God and not the world; and finally, don't nurture the bad that is already there—get rid of it.

We need to read and actively meditate on the Bible. Yes, I said it, practice meditation.

One of the best things to happen to me as a new believer was being told that "all Christians memorize Scripture through meditation." By the time I found out biblical meditation wasn't so widespread, I was hooked. I've been practicing meditation for several years now and, trust me, it has served me well. You see, I believe that just as your digestive system processes food so that it can be used as energy, meditation digests all things concerning God and makes them a power that can renew your heart and mind.

The Word of God plays a central role in meditation because it is the place where our knowledge of God originates. We can release trauma and stress there. We can envision better living and have a clearer view of what we want from life and what we should pursue. We can focus on better living and freedom from addictions, fear, and other oppressive behaviors. We can even enjoy interaction with the Holy Spirit of God through faithful and focused meditation. All we need to do is want it! Want a better life . . . want to live beyond the constraints of this world . . . want to live in the peace of God . . . want fruitfulness in our lives . . . want a life that makes sense . . . and want to *receive* God's best!

There is no single way to meditate, but in the devotional study at the end of the book, I present some suggestions for Christian meditation. A good focus point to start with is Joshua 1:8 (NKJV), which reminds us that memorizing Scripture facilitates meditation:

> This Book of the Law shall not depart from your mouth, but you shall meditate in it day and night, that you may observe to do according to all that is written in it. For then you will make your way prosperous, and then you will have good success.

Ah, yes, if you want the formula for genuine prosperity, there it is!

An Afterthought

It is my sincere prayer that together we have explored how to make sense of a senseless world. Through each chapter of this book, I have tried to convey how important it is to seek to know God through His written Word and prayer. Once we know God, we can know ourselves. And in knowing ourselves we begin to live life fully through service to God by utilizing our gifts and fighting against the enemies of our soul in whatever form—our flesh, the world, or the devil himself—to take back our earth and deliver God's ultimate purpose.

We change our lives by changing our character and living the peace of God through faith that keeps us moving forward through crises, through false hope, through loneliness, drugs, depression, financial crisis, and other life issues, through apostasy and even through these end times to reach our ultimate goal: finding ourselves in the presence of God for all eternity, reunited with our lost garden and uninterrupted in our fellowship with our Creator. And this is what makes it all make sense. It's what we live for!

Reflection—the Real Me

Your character is being formed and solidified every day of your life. This is true whether you are proactive with your life or if you just sit back and let things happen. Every day, powerful external character-building influences are shaping you—from media and people around you to the Bible. Whose "hands" (what things) are forming your heart and mind?

An Offered Prayer

Lord,

You are the potter and I am the clay. Make me into the person of your vision. Help me, Lord, to be active in my life and who I am. Place in me a desire to meditate on your words and change my way of thinking to yours. Amen.

21

What Does It Mean to Be Born Again?

Life Is More Than a Beating Heart

"The thief cometh not, but for to steal, and to kill, and to destroy: I am come that they might have life, and that they might have it more abundantly."

—John 10:10 KJV

I hope all this makes sense to you. I hope that from the beginning to the end of this book the pieces have come together and you can clearly see God's perfect plan for our lives, our earth, and all of His creation. Life really does make perfect sense when lived according to the system that He has set before us and in the shadow of His wings.

We were created for God's purpose, which was established before time. The enemy met us in the garden and deceived us

195

to prevent God's plan, but it didn't work. God sent His Son Jesus Christ to die on a cross, and when time is finished and God's purpose is revealed through us, we will have completed God's plan. Satan and his legions will be cast into a fiery hell and evil will be banished from the earth forever. No more sin. Hallelujah!

In the meantime, we live.

And as we wait for that appointed time, we embrace the peace that God gives through all the slings and arrows of outrageous fortune, all the senseless acts of sin, the brokenness, and every great and small change in our life journeys. Change is good!

I must admit it gets difficult at times—to always go gracefully and give thanks to God in all things. It's a stretch to count all of it as joy, right?

If I could, there might be some things in my life that I would change to make things easier. But to what end? What does Leslie look like without 9/11, or a tumor, or heartbreak, or any other circumstance that God has given me the strength to overcome? What is my service like without being silly and introverted and assertive and cerebral and happy and sad and all the things He designed me to be?

Honestly, at this place in my journey with Him, I really do look forward to the surprises and I consider it joy that He is my partner through it all. I can't wait to see Him. I can't wait to hear Him speak in audible tones that register to my awareness. What a sweet sound. I look forward to the seat on my front porch in heaven, where my tall glass of lemonade awaits with the friendships of the apostle Paul, Jonah, Job, Deborah, Sarah, Mary, my mom and dad, my cousin Randy, my grandparents, Lisa . . . and, oh yeah, Eve.

And that's the secret to making sense of life—living toward the end goal, outside the purview of this world. Any other way loses sight of the plan. Otherwise we're just taking the computer apart without the knowledge of the designer's specifications. Otherwise we get stuck in the moment and forget that it doesn't end here. Where it ends for you, however, is *your* choice.

So, it wouldn't be a Leslie Haskin book if we did not come to this place. This is where I invite you, if you haven't done so already, to believe that Jesus Christ is who *He* says that He is and accept His offer of salvation and God's gift of eternal life with Him.

How do you do that?

Salvation is very simple—we are sinners, and Jesus rescues or "saves" us from sin and hell. All we have to do is believe that and then ask Him to take over our hearts, live with us, and make us new. That's being born again. Anyone who believes Jesus for salvation becomes a part of God's family (Romans 10:13; Galatians 3:26).

You see, friend, there is no religion involved here, only Jesus.

So then, are you ready to receive Jesus Christ as your personal Savior? Are you ready to be born again into the family of God? Are you ready to have a place in heaven for all eternity?

If you are, just close your eyes and talk to Him. Tell Him about your heart. Tell Him about your fears and your life. And ask Him to give you a new life in Jesus Christ. He will by His Holy Spirit.

Pause here. Reflect on your decision.

If you have invited Jesus Christ to come into your life, I'd love to personally welcome you to the family, so gimme a shout on Facebook! Otherwise, I'll save a seat for ya on my front porch.

I pray God's richest blessing for your life in the in-betweens . . .

Please join me in prayer for those who do not yet know Christ as Savior and Lord. Feel free to send names to: praying fornewlife@gmail.com and join our Facebook page, "100 day Journey."

It really is a matter of life or death.

Leslie

Devotional Studies

"Of these things put them in remembrance, charging
them before the Lord that they strive not about words
to no profit, but to the subverting of the hearers. Study
to shew thyself approved unto God, a workman that
needeth not to be ashamed, rightly dividing the word
of truth."

—2 Timothy 2:14–15 KJV

The Bible tells us to study and know God's Word for ourselves. The following devotional studies are designed to help
you do just that—study and rightly divide the Word of truth.
In each section, you will find questions to stir deeper thought,
additional reading for more understanding, and exercises to
help you practice what you've learned.

Discuss them in a small group, book club, or Sunday school
class, or simply use them for your own personal daily time
with God. Whatever way you choose to use them, I encourage you to take the time to go through each study before you

move on to the next section of the book. Pause and listen for the voice of God in your life. Don't rush through it, even if you end up taking a week or two to finish.

It is through our study that God gives deeper revelation into His Word, and through prayer that we find intimacy with our Father.

Selah

SECTION ONE—
Knowing God

"There is a God-shaped vacuum in the heart of every man, which cannot be filled by any created thing, but only by God, the Creator, made known through Jesus."

—Blaise Pascal

Our Christian journey depends on our relationship with God and how we relate to Him. Relating to Him is about understanding His attributes, our communication with Him, and the amount of time that we spend with Him in prayer and in His written Word.

This devotional study, based on section 1 of the book, focuses on hearing from God. It is designed to help you know God better and regularly communicate with Him more effectively in order to model your life to His likeness. We do this by looking deeper into the character and power of God and communicating with Him.

201

The Character of God

- Read Genesis 1
- Read John 1

In many ways the statement that God is light is the main theme that flows throughout the New Testament. It includes a definition of God's character as well as implications for the life of Christian discipleship. In fact, to describe the character of God as light and Christian life as "walking in the light" is the whole point.

So when we say to someone, "God is light," it doesn't come as much of a surprise. No one can argue that the greatest power and greatest good in the world is God, and He is the essence of light.

Questions for Deeper Reflection

1. In chapter 1, we talk about how *light* was the first word God uttered. Reflect on or discuss its literal and symbolic meanings.
   a. What is the main function of light?
   b. Discuss the attributes of God within your group; think about which aspect of God's character is most prevalent at different times in your life—during a difficult time, during a time of celebration, etc.
   c. How does knowing the attributes of God enhance your awareness of His power and His presence?
2. God speaks to us in many different ways, yet we often put Him in a box and only look for Him through His Word and through sermons. Chapter 3 explored God

speaking through a text message. Share any unconventional ways you believe God has spoken to you.

   a. How have you put God in a box, and how do you hear Him speak to you?

   b. It's be-honest time. Do you believe God speaks through technology?

3. Your answer to who God is will also give insight into who you are in Him. Talk about or reflect on how that works.

   a. Who do you believe you are in Christ? How does Scripture define believers?

4. In many ways, knowing the names of God will reveal His power. His attributes provide deeper insight into the character of God. Describe the power of God in your life and tie it to one of His attributes.

   a. Does this attribute give you more confidence in Him? How?

Exercises for Growth

In the names of God, the word *El* comes from the root word meaning "might, strength, power." Memorize the names of God to know His character better. Can you add three other characteristics not listed here—ways God has shown himself to you? For example, I believe silence is another characteristic of God. Many of us have experienced His silence when we desired to hear Him most.

The Names of God

1. **El:** God (mighty, strong, prominent)
2. **Elohim:** God—plural of "El"—God as Creator, Preserver, transcendent

3. **El Shaddai:** The All-Sufficient God
4. **El-Berith:** The God of the Covenant
5. **El-Chad:** The One God
6. **El-Chaiyia:** The God of My Life
7. **El De'ot:** The God of Knowledge
8. **El Elyon:** The Most High God
9. **El Emet:** The God of Truth
10. **El Gibhor:** The Mighty God, God the Warrior
11. **El Hanne'eman:** The Faithful God
12. **El Haggado:** The Great God
13. **El Hakkavod:** The God of Glory
14. **El Hakkadosh:** The Holy God
15. **El Olam:** The Everlasting God
16. **El Rachum:** The God of Compassion
17. **El Roi:** The God Who Sees Me or the God Who Opens Our Eyes
18. **El Sali:** The God of My Strength
19. **El Tsaddik:** The Righteous God
20. **El Yeshuatia:** The God of My Salvation
21. **Attiz Yomin** (Aramaic): Ancient of Days, Messiah, The Sun of Righteousness, Wonderful, Counselor (pele' ya'ats), Mighty God
22. **Kadosh:** Holy One
23. **Shaphat:** Judge

Communicating With God

- Read Acts 2

Communication is one of God's fields of light, and the children of light walk in it daily. In biblical thought, *walking* is a synonym for living (Proverbs 6:23; Psalm 1). So to say that we as followers of Jesus Christ *walk in the light* is another way of saying that the Christian life is lived in God's light and in communication with Him. In openly communicating with God, we are able to discern and follow the way of righteousness and truth that is salvation and life. C. S. Lewis said, "We believe that the sun is in the sky at midday in summer not because we can clearly see the sun (in fact, we cannot) but because we can see everything else." Communicating with God is like that. We cannot see the light, but in and through the light we see everything else.

Questions for Deeper Reflection

1. Prayer is a fundamental way to get to know God better, of communicating with Him, and of walking in the light. But it is important to remember first that prayer involves listening.
   a. What is your prayer life like? Is it mostly talking to God, or do you listen as well? How do you listen to Him?
   b. Are you open to experiencing God and enjoying His presence even in unconventional ways? Describe a time in your life that God spoke in an unexpected or unconventional way.
2. Are you responding to all He desires for you? What are your passions?

Exercises for Growth

Prayer is one of the most effective ways of communicating with God, but not just in running our mouths off, spouting the long list of things for God to do. In fact, I believe prayer is more about positioning ourselves to hear.

Lectio Divina is Latin for "spiritual reading" or "holy reading." It is an ancient prayer practice that helps many people encounter the living God through His written Word. In Lectio Divina, we come with open hearts and without an agenda, quieting our hearts and minds and turning our focus to God.

Let's practice.

FIND SOLITUDE

Make yourself comfortable in a place that will be free from interruptions—so you can be alone with God. My mother's favorite spot was her bathroom, in the tub for hours. For me, I like to work in my garden or go on a hike; my son, Eliot, simply goes into his studio space and closes the door with a towel underneath it. The objective is simply to listen. Have one word in your mind, and look around you and listen to the thoughts that come to mind. It is especially helpful to be alone in nature, as God speaks so clearly and powerfully to us through His creation. But remember, God's voice comes first.

PREPARE YOURSELF

Quiet yourself before God. Quiet your heart and mind and turn your focus to God. When I do it, it helps me to remember that I am entering into the presence of the living God, who is HERE . . . present with me. I actually envision myself walking into the throne room of God. If you do that, you can't help but change how you behave and how you speak.

LISTEN AND RESPOND

Our prayers are a response to God, not the other way around. Be silent for a few minutes, humbly asking God to quiet your heart and make you aware that you are in His loving presence. Let everything else go, as best as you can, and wait.

READ AND VISUALIZE

Begin to read the Bible and listen for His voice. Read for the story and the message, not the words. Try to focus on the big picture. When I read the Bible, I try to understand the times, what the people wore, and how they lived. It helps me to hear their perspective in the writing.

One of my favorite stories to read is when Jesus drove the money changers out of the temple. In my mind's eye, I see Him standing by, watching, and perfectly timing His actions. My lesson in that story is to control myself and my response to things that happen around me. Consequently, I am a lot less reactionary.

HEAR AND PRAY

As you read the Bible, allow yourself to visualize the passage and then ask yourself, What am I thinking about this? How is it making me feel? What thoughts are coming to my mind? This is the voice of God. Write it down and apply it to your life.

NOW PRAY—EXPRESS YOUR HONEST HEART TO GOD

Tell Him what you just read and what you believe He is saying to you through His Word. Ask Him to speak to you. Tell Him of your joys and struggles, your hopes and fears. Humbly ask on behalf of others first, and then ask for the things you need. Then sit quietly and listen, again. Take your listening heart out and into your day.

FINALLY, WATCH

As you go about your day, pay attention to all the ways God speaks to you about the very things you were thinking as you read from His Word. You're gonna love it!

Understanding Me

"Man is to himself the most wonderful object in nature; for he cannot conceive what the body is, still less what the mind is, and least of all how a body should be united to a mind. This is the consummation of his difficulties, and yet it is his very being."

—Blaise Pascal, *Pensées* (II, 72)

As we begin to know God better, we also know ourselves better. He strips away the layers of iniquity and opens our eyes to the enemy's deception. In doing so, He brings to fruition His vision for our lives. While many of us take shortcuts, the fulfillment of our dreams and our destiny takes time.

This section's devotional study is designed to help you understand who you are in Christ and what He wants from you. In order to accomplish that, we look deeper into *What Is Man?* and *Ministry and Service*.

What Is Man?

- Read Genesis 1–6
- Read Psalm 8

In Psalm 8:4, David asks God: "What is man, that thou art mindful of him? and the son of man, that thou visitest him?" (KJV). There are literally thousands of books that attempt to answer that question. Most focus on our creation purpose and not our worth to God. And I agree that in order to understand our value and who we are in Christ, we must first understand our purpose, or what we were created to do for Him.

In Hebrew thought, existence is a result of purpose. Nothing exists unless it serves a specific function in God's order. God's decision to make human beings came from His purpose.

Genesis talks about our purpose as well as our works. According to Genesis, Adam was placed in the garden and told to do a work of restoration on the earth because it had been taken over by Satan. And in order for man to successfully get it back, God created man in His image and His likeness. Our soul was created by God as a vessel to contain His mind, will, and emotion (see Matthew 22:37; Ephesians 5:17; Colossians 1:9–10).

As spirit beings, when God created Adam, He wanted him to deal with His enemy. This is man's purpose.

Questions for Deeper Reflection

1. In chapter 9, we looked at our value and the gifts God has entrusted to us. If man's value is equal to his purpose

in God, how would you answer David's question in Psalm 8?

 a. How do our gifts support this belief?

 b. What works are evidentially tied to our purpose?

 c. Reflect on or talk about the importance of who you are in Christ and the authority God has given you. How did He prepare you to fulfill His purpose?

 d. What are your individual gifts?

 e. Reflect on or discuss ways to use your gifts to take care of the earth, family, relationships, health, and finances.

2. Chapter 12 is all about hope and faith. The belief is that one cannot exist without the other. In your opinion, what is it about faith that causes us to hope?

 a. What are some examples of false hope?

 b. Have there been situations where you were holding on when you should have been letting go? What are some of the dangers of false hope?

Exercises for Growth

The following is a short list of spiritual gifts (and definitions) from 1 Corinthians 12:7–10. Read over them and identify the areas in which you are gifted. Later, we will tie those gifts to areas of ministry.

Keep in mind that your gifts will follow your purpose. They will be in the areas of your works or service. For example, I never tire of speaking to people about the Lord, and I get fighting mad at even the thought of someone dying at the hands of the enemy. After studying the gifts, I found that God often uses me in the areas of healing, evangelism, and discerning of spirits.

SPIRITUAL GIFTS

There isn't agreement as to the precise nature of each of the gifts of the Spirit, but here is a list.

The Gift of Administration is the ability to keep things organized and in accordance with God's principles.

The Gift of Celibacy or Singleness is the divine enablement to some members of the body of Christ to remain single and enjoy it, to be unmarried and not suffer from sexual temptations.

The Gift of Compassion is the divine ability to feel intense compassion for others and help those who are suffering or are in need by putting faith and compassion into action.

The Gift of Discerning Spirits is the ability to determine whether or not a message, person, or event is truly from God and recognize the spirit behind it.

The Gift of Discernment is the divine ability to clearly distinguish truth from error by judging whether the behavior or teaching is from God, Satan, human error, or human power.

The Gift of Evangelism is the ability and desire to boldly and clearly communicate the gospel of Jesus Christ so that non-Christians can become Christians.

The Gift of Exhortation is the ability to present truth so as to strengthen or urge to action those who are discouraged or wavering in their faith.

The Gift of Faith is being able to stand steadfast on God's Word and to trust God and encourage others to trust God, no matter the circumstances.

The Gift of Giving is the ability to cheerfully and liberally share monetary or material gifts with others without expecting reciprocity.

The Gift of Healing is the miraculous ability to use God's healing power to restore a person who is sick, injured, or suffering (physically, emotionally, mentally, or spiritually).

The Gift of Helps is always having the desire and ability to help or serve others, to do whatever it takes to get a task accomplished.

The Gift of Hospitality is the ability to genuinely care for people by providing fellowship, food, and shelter, even to strangers.

The Gift of Interpreting Tongues is the ability to interpret the tongue being spoken and communicate it back to others in your own language.

The Gift of Knowledge is the ability to have an in-depth understanding of a spiritual issue or situation and help to guide others.

The Gift of Leadership is the ability to set goals in accordance with God's purpose and to cast vision, motivate, and direct people to harmoniously accomplish the purposes of God.

The Gift of Martyrdom is the ability to sacrifice one's own life for the cause of Christ.

The Gift of Miracles is being able to perform signs and wonders that give authenticity to God's Word and the gospel message.

The Gift of Missionary is the ability to be comfortably led to other cultures to serve.

The Gift of Music is the ability to present personal witness and inspiration to others through instrumental music, singing, or dancing in a way that the hearers also hear and feel the presence of God. (Sometimes healings take place with this gift.)

The Gift of Poverty is the special ability that God gives to some people to be able to comfortably renounce material luxury and adopt a personal lifestyle equivalent to those living at the poverty level in order to serve that group of people more effectively for God.

The Gift of Prophecy is being able to proclaim a message from God.

The Gift of Service is the ability to see concrete, practical work that needs to be done for groups or programs to function, and volunteer to do it.

The Gift of Teaching is the ability to understand, clearly explain, and apply the Word of God, causing greater Christlikeness in the lives of listeners.

The Gift of Tongues is the ability to speak in a foreign language that you do not have knowledge of in order to communicate a message to the church, provided there is interpretation, or to simply worship God in private when your own words fail you.

The Gift of Wisdom is the ability to make decisions and give guidance that is according to God's will.

The Gift of Writing is the God-given ability to formulate thoughts and ideas into meaningful written forms so that the reader will find courage, guidance, knowledge, or edification through the words shared with them.

Ministry and Service

- Read Isaiah 58
- Read 1 Corinthians

Each of you should use whatever gift you have received to serve others, as faithful stewards of God's grace in its various forms.

—1 Peter 4:10

Spiritual gifts are enablement for ministry given by the Holy Spirit to all believers and are to be used to build and serve the body of Christ. Knowing what your gifts are will help you find God's personal plan for your life. As you approach ministry, pray for guidance about your spiritual gift(s), and ask people you trust and who know you what they think your gifts are. (Discuss in your group.)

The pieces fit together like a well-planned machine to make a whole. When you combine your spiritual gifts, personality, passions, and experience, you will discover a picture that shows you how you were built to individually serve the Lord. Each part of who you are affects the other parts and contributes to how God wants to use you.

Your purpose inspires your relationship with God. Your relationship with God motivates you for ministry, your spiritual gifts enable you for ministry, your passions give focus to your ministry, your personality expresses itself in ministry, and your experiences prepare you for ministry.

As you decide where to best put your gifts to service, avoid the common pitfalls and delay tactics that the enemy will use to keep you from God's work. There are six I see often. *Do not:*

1. Continuously look for signs from dreams or people
2. Over-spiritualize the decision
3. Sit idly by, waiting for God to make the choice for you, or just keep praying about it
4. Simply wait for the right doors to open and the wrong doors to close
5. Ask a church leader to make a decision for you
6. Believe that you have no gifts and have not been chosen by God for service

Questions for Deeper Reflection

1. What exactly is the nature and purpose of the filling of the Spirit? Is it enablement for service, or is its design for the sanctification of the believer?
2. In the book of Acts, the filling of the Spirit is clearly seen as God's enablement for service and for witness and proclamation of the gospel of the Lord Jesus Christ (see Acts 4:8; 9:17; 11:24; 13:9, 52). How is the Spirit seen in today's church?
3. It is important to identify your gifts and then use them in ministry. This is one way to honor God. What are other ways to honor God in service?
    a. Reflect on or talk about what you wanted to be when you were a child and what your passions are now. How have they changed?
    b. Reflect on or talk about your personality and how comfortable you are in your skin. How do your gifts serve God's purpose?
4. We know that everyone who is a believer is called to spread the gospel message, so everyone must have the gift of evangelism, or at least some capability of sharing

it. What other universal missions and gifts can you identify?

  a. How do these gifts make sense during these days and which ones are of greater use?

5. Chapter 10 talks about our relationship with God, ministry, and how we often substitute things for our desire to be with God.

  a. Are you replacing God's love with cheap substitutes? Is it with more stuff? A puffed-up ego? Unhealthy relationships? Food?

  b. How have your human love experiences shaped your view of God's love? Commit to separate God from the actions of humans today and accept His love.

  c. How has God proven faithful to you throughout your life?

  d. How have you responded to God's faithfulness in your life? Are you living the mission (or calling) of your life?

Exercises for Growth

The list of spiritual gifts earlier in this section is not intended to be an exhaustive or all-inclusive list. I encourage you to extend your study to find your good fit. Several websites such as Ministry Tools Resource Center (http://mintools.com/gifts-list.htm) and (www.kodachrome.org/spiritgift/) have more comprehensive lists and occupations that fit well with certain gifts, training for teachers, and small-group leaders, as well as educational programs for all ages.

Have someone who knows you well match your gifts and skills to possible ministry areas. Talk about what you have learned about yourself and how you fit in ministry. *Challenge*

Exercise: Volunteer for ten days of ministry work in the areas where you feel led. Share your experience with family, friends, and your church. Again, talk about what you have learned.

Seek God's face as you go forth and "May the God of peace . . . equip you with everything good for doing His will" (Hebrews 13:20-21).

The Church and the World

"Men despise religion; they hate it and fear it is true. To remedy this, we must begin by showing that religion is not contrary to reason; that it is venerable, to inspire respect for it; then we must make it lovable, to make good men hope it is true; finally, we must prove it is true. Venerable, because it has perfect knowledge of man; lovable because it promises the true good."

—Blaise Pascal

In Jewish tradition, the purpose of a synagogue is in its name, "house of prayer," which is closely related to house of worship. And in the Christian tradition, our purpose is also found in the Greek word *koinonia,* usually translated as "fellowship community" or "community of sharing." Believers gather for prayer, worship, community, outreach (evangelism), community service, etc. But our purpose should always be theocentric or God-centered, meaning to worship the Trinity: Father, Son, and Holy Spirit.

In this final section of devotional study, our objective is to get a clearer understanding of the signs and times we live in, the role of the church in the last days, and how it fits into God's ultimate plan.

As I begin to write this final section, I do so with a spirit of heaviness. Why? Because this study focuses on a teaching I want to expose that is held in high regard by so many Christians and is taught by so many able and respected leaders.

I approach the subject not only with deep concern but also great caution. "He who has ears to hear, let him hear."

The Biblical Purpose of the Church and Its Mission

- Read 2 Timothy
- Read 1 Corinthians 4
- Read Acts 1
- Read Matthew 24

The church is generally seen in two ways: the visible and the invisible. The visible church is made up of everyone who attends services and professes to be a Christian. While their roles are about attendance only, this is where most of the emphasis seems to be these days.

The invisible church consists of those who are truly born again and who trust in Christ by faith alone. And just as arms and legs are members of a human body with different functions, the invisible church, also known as the body of Christ, uses its various gifts and talents to serve Christ in various ways. Inspired by the Holy Spirit of God, it leads the lost to Christ and spreads the message of the gospel around the world. This is about people. It's the mission of the church.

Though there isn't a single verse that precisely defines the purpose of the church, Acts 2:42 gives a good summary: "They were continually devoting themselves to the apostles' teaching and to fellowship, to the breaking of bread and to prayer." This is all about God and who He is, including His body, the church.

The bottom line is that the church has many missions, but just one purpose.

Questions for Deeper Reflection

1. Chapter 15 talks about man's purpose, and chapter 18 talks about the purpose of the church.
   a. What is the difference between the mission of the church and the mission of the believer?
   b. Discuss the purpose of the true church and examine yourself and/or your church in that light. How do you fare? Are you stuck in mission mode, or are you fulfilling the purpose?
2. In chapters 19 and 20, we talk about the last days and the signs of the times. Review the discussion about churches that are falling away from Christ.
   a. In what ways have you witnessed churches that are falling away, and what can you do as a part of the body of Christ to help restore them?
3. In chapter 19 we review several signs of the end times. Matthew 24 also talks about the last days. Reflect and discuss:
   a. How does the kingdom gospel in Matthew differ from the watered-down "gospel" preached in some churches today?

b. How has the church witnessed "the increase of lawlessness," causing "most people's love [to] grow cold" (v. 12)?

c. How can you prevent your love from growing cold so that you can continue to share in God's heart?

d. Are you timid when it comes to sharing your faith with others? Do you consider it old-fashioned to talk about heaven and hell? How can you challenge yourself to be bold in your proclamation of the gospel message?

Exercises for Growth

As believers, we should always be prepared to speak about our faith and defend the position of the body of Christ, the true church. Memorize the mission of the church below. Make a list of others that you can think of. Be sure to apply biblical passages.

MISSION OF THE CHURCH

- **To become more like Christ:** "Instead, speaking the truth in love, we will grow to become in every respect the mature body of him who is the head, that is, Christ" (Ephesians 4:15–16).

- **To preach the gospel to the world:** "And he said unto them, Go ye into all the world, and preach the gospel to every creature" (Mark 16:15 KJV).

- **To guard the proper teachings of the church:** "You then, my son, be strong in the grace that is in Christ Jesus. And the things you have heard me say in the presence of many witnesses entrust to reliable people who will also be qualified to teach others" (2 Timothy 2:1–2).

- **To be subject to pastoral leadership and to lead:** "To the elders among you, I appeal as a fellow elder and a witness of Christ's sufferings who also will share in the glory to be revealed: Be shepherds of God's flock that is under your care, watching over them—not because you must, but because you are willing, as God wants you to be; not pursuing dishonest gain, but eager to serve; not lording it over those entrusted to you, but being examples to the flock" (1 Peter 5:1–3).

- **To be unified in Christ:** "There is neither Jew nor Gentile, neither slave nor free, nor is there male and female, for you are all one in Christ Jesus"(Galatians 3:28).

The World's View (Love Not the World)

- Read 1 Peter
- Read Titus 2
- Read 1 John 2

According to *Easton's Revised Bible Dictionary,* the title *Christian* was most likely given by the Romans in reproach to the followers of Jesus. But the disciples were known to one another as *believer, brethren, the faithful, elect, saints.* They were known by their faith and service to Jesus. But as their faith became more widely known, in order to distinguish them from the multitude, the name *Christian* came into use and was universally accepted.

The question is, what was so different about the followers of Jesus that called for them to be resented by the community they lived in? Could it be many of the people didn't want anything to do with the godliness and separation that these followers displayed? Many people of the time lived carnal lives, meaning they wanted God, but held on to the sins of the flesh and the standards set by the world. This is the world's view.

In the suggested readings, you'll find the writer refers to Christians as being a "peculiar" people. But *peculiar* doesn't just mean "strange," it also means "chosen, selected, unique." God has selected us for great and marvelous works, chosen "out of the world."

Being peculiar people in this sense is to be true followers of Jesus, seeking what God wants to do with our lives. Usually that goes against the world's view. A true Christian is ready to give up everything because of God and live in total obedience and submission to Him all the time; that most certainly goes against the world's view. And manifesting a life in Christ means a Christian must turn from pride, anger, and materialistic pursuits and be ready to let go of everything for the sake of the kingdom of God.

Questions for Deeper Reflection

1. Throughout the book, we talked about moving beyond our flesh or carnality and living by faith, getting to know God and living according to His will for our lives. Can a true Christian be carnal?
   a. How is the great apostasy evidence of a growing population of carnal living and acceptance of the world's standards?
2. Many Christians have problems because they are living carnal lives for the most part, or living out the gospel only halfway. How have you separated yourself from the world's system?
3. We read that as a result of erroneous teaching, many people who regularly occupy our church pews on

Sunday morning and fill our church rolls are strangers to true conversion. Reflect on or talk about how the enemy has deceived people into bad behaviors without repentance.

    a. What are a few of those behaviors, and what does God want us to do about it? How can you live in response to the condition of the church today without compromising your beliefs?

4. Chapter 17 told us that we must be mindful of false doctrine and study God's Word for ourselves. In Hebrews 13:9, it says, "Do not be carried away by all kinds of strange teachings." Another translation puts it like this: "So do not be swept off your course by all sorts of outlandish teaching." Yet another says, "So do not be attracted by strange, new ideas."

    a. How can we guard against believing whatever we hear from false teachers?

5. Meditation is a function of the mind and the heart. It is what we think about in our hearts every day. Whether we realize it or not, we all spend a large portion of our time in some form of meditation. What things do you ponder throughout the day?

    a. How is your behavior impacted?

    b. How often do you re-live the bad things people do or say to you, and do you list your misfortunes?

    c. Do you allow yourself to be angry for long periods of time?

6. If we really are the sum of the things that we think about, how would you describe yourself based on your thought life?

    a. What does the "you" of God's vision look like?

Exercises for Growth

Over the next few days, take special note of the things you spend your time thinking about. Consider the following questions.

- Where does your mind wander to?
- What thoughts are constant and what areas of thought are forced?
- Based on your thoughts, what is the condition of your heart?

Challenge Exercise: The Bible tells us, for the sake of engraving God's Word on the tablets of our heart, to meditate on the Word of God day and night. For many of us with hectic, stressful lives, the extent of our meditation is zoning out in front of the TV at the end of the day or sleeping in over the weekend. Unfortunately, this does little to help us to change our thought lives and live more productively—the way that God intended. Meditation is a key to changing our thought lives. Let's practice.

Steps in Christian Meditation

- Take a comfortable seated position with a straight spine and shoulders back.
- Relax all of your muscles. Close your eyes and begin breathing through your nose. Notice if your breath is shallow and confined to your upper chest area.
- On your inhalation, bring the breath down to the belly. Fill up the belly with your breath, as if you're filling up a balloon and then expand your chest. On the inhalation, lengthen your spine and rise up.

- On your exhalation, you contract—your belly and chest go toward the spine as if you are deflating a balloon.
- Inhale for a count of four seconds, hold your breath for four seconds, and exhale for six seconds. Repeat this breathing for a few minutes. If your mind wanders, gently guide it back to your exercise.
- Visualize God in His throne room.
- See yourself walking toward Him with all of your life issues in your hands. Now humbly bow down in front of Him and place your issues at His feet, one at a time. (You can say them out loud if you like.)
- Feel yourself getting lighter as each burden is laid down.
- Now visualize your life without those problems. (Allow the Holy Spirit of God to give you the vision.)
- Now speak words of affirmation and praise as God shows you His vision for you.
- Allow the peace of God to overtake you.
- Relax. Repeat the breathing exercise.

TIPS FOR MEDITATION

1. **A quiet environment.** Choose a secluded place in your home, office, garden, place of worship, or in the great outdoors where you can relax without distractions or interruptions.
2. **A comfortable position.** Get comfortable, but avoid lying down as this may lead to falling asleep! Sit up with your spine straight, either in a chair or on the floor. You can also try sitting cross-legged.
3. **A point of focus.** This point can be internal and a place of safety and resolve. Never focus on a problem. Always focus on the solution.

4. **An observant, noncritical attitude.** Don't worry about distracting thoughts that go through your mind or about how well you're doing. If thoughts intrude during your relaxation session, don't fight them. Instead, gently turn your attention back to your point of focus.

OTHER POINTS OF FOCUS

- The things God has done for you and others you know
- The holiness and perfection of God
- The beauty of Christ
- Your meeting with God after your life here is complete
- The eternal fellowship you will one day have with Him
- The meaning/application of any specific passage of Scripture
- Anything God has recently taught you or made you aware of
- Questions regarding the will of God
- The salvation He has given you

Notes

Section One: Knowing God

1. Arthur G. Bennett, editor, *The Valley of Vision* (Carlisle, PA: Banner of Truth, 1975) as quoted at www.banneroftruth.org/pages/daily devotion_detail.php?898, accessed May 2, 2012.

Chapter 5: How Can I Read Your Word and Still Not Find Help? KJV, NKJV, and NIV . . . It's All Greek to Me

1. A. W. Tozer, *The Pursuit of God* (Rockville, MD: Serenity Publishers, 2009), 17–18.

Section Two: Understanding Me

1. A. W. Tozer, compiled from *Rut, Rot or Revival* (Camp Hill, PA: Christian Publications, 1992), chap. 11, as quoted at www.cmalliance.org/devotions/tozer?id=381.

Chapter 10: Why Am I Still Single? Relationship Status—"It's Complicated"

1. From the movie *He's Just Not That Into You*, 2010.

Chapter 11: Why Do I Feel So Lonely? Twitterpated

1. Quote from the movie *Practical Magic*.

Notes

Section Three: The Church and the World

1. A. W. Tozer, compiled from *Rut, Rot or Revival*, chap. 11, "Two Portraits of the Church," quoted at www.cmalliance.org/devotions/tozer ?id=382.

2. Edward G. Bennett, editor, *The Valley of Vision*, quoted at www. spurgeongems.org/prayers.htm.

Chapter 13: As Christians, Aren't We Supposed to Prosper? The Means or the End

1. A. W. Tozer, compiled from *Renewed Day by Day*, Vol. 2 (Camp Hill, PA: Christian Publications, 1991), quoted at www.cmalliance.org/ devotions/tozer?id=287.

Chapter 14: If God Is In Control, Why Does Everything Seem So Out of Control? "I AM"

1. A. W. Tozer, compiled from *The Knowledge of the Holy* (New York: HarperOne, 1978), quoted at www.cmalliance.org/devotions/tozer ?id=1429.

2. Arthur W. Pink, *The Sovereignty of God* (Grand Rapids, MI: Baker Book House, 1984), 240.

3. Edwin H. Palmer, *The Five Points of Calvinism* (Grand Rapids, MI: Baker Books, 1999), 25.

Chapter 16: Is Hell Real? The Reality of Eternity . . . Under Fire!

1. J. P. Moreland, quoted by Lee Strobel, *The Case for Faith* (Grand Rapids, MI: Zondervan, 2000), 174.

2. Maurice Rawlings, *Beyond Death's Door* (Nashville, TN: Thomas Nelson, 1979), 3.

Leslie Haskin has become the voice of hope for many. Known for her miraculous escape from the World Trade Center on September 11, 2001, her testimony of climbing the corporate ladder and then losing it all is both engaging and heartrending. Even more compelling is God's faithfulness in transforming her life.

Today, Leslie is active in outreach ministry and is the founding director of Safe Hugs Ministries, an agency that helps women and children. She is the author of three previous books: *Between Heaven and Ground Zero, Held,* and *God Has Not Forgotten About You.* Leslie travels internationally, spreading a message of hope and overcoming, and has been featured on *The 700 Club,* CNN, *Good Morning America,* Moody Radio, and other media outlets. She makes her home in upstate New York.

To learn more about Leslie, or to schedule her to speak at your next event, visit www.lesliehaskin.net.

A Message of Hope—
Especially for You

When everyday concerns and problems linger—when desires of our heart go unmet—it's easy to wonder if we've done something wrong or if God cares.

Leslie Haskin is no stranger to these feelings, but through adversity she has emerged victorious.

"This book is honest and straightforward. It is about real life for real people," Leslie says. "Whether the struggle is emotional, spiritual, or physical, I write for those who, like me, would like some answers but even more need a revival of spirit.

"Nothing in our lives is too small for God, so be encouraged in your walk with Him today. You indeed can make it to the other side of whatever you are facing and be better for the experience. I assure you, God loves you more than you can imagine."

God Has Not Forgotten About You by Leslie Haskin

◊ BETHANYHOUSE

 Stay up-to-date on your favorite books and authors with our *free* e-newsletters. Sign up today at *bethanyhouse.com*.

 Find us on Facebook.